GENERATIVE COACHING

Volume 1

The Journey of Creative and Sustainable Change

International Association for Generative Change

114 Ponderosa Drive

Santa Cruz, CA 95060

USA

E-Mail: info@generative-change.com

Homepage: https://generative-change.com/

Library of Congress Control Number: 2021907725

I.S.B.N. 978-0-578-89696-0

GENERATIVE COACHING
Volume 1
The Journey of Creative and Sustainable Change

Robert B. Dilts

Stephen Gilligan

Design and illustrations: Antonio Meza

TABLE OF CONTENTS

TABLE OF CONTENTS

TABLE OF CONTENTS

We would like to dedicate this book to our mutual mentors Milton H. Erickson and Gregory Bateson. May the generous and generative spirit that they awakened in us continue to live on through this work.

Milton H. Erickson

Gregory Bateson

* Drawings by Robert Dilts

Acknowledgments

We would like to gratefully acknowledge our sponsors around the world who have embraced our Generative Coaching work and provided a platform for us to share it with so many others.

We equally want to acknowledge the many students who have participated in helping us develop this work, especially those who participated in the demonstrations of the key steps of the process.

We also acknowledge all of the members of the International Association for Generative Change who have joined us in brining this dream to a reality including our fellow teachers, professional members, associate members and other participants in the IAGC community who are passionate about the work.

We want to express our gratitude to Nick LeForce, whose poems open five of the chapters of this book. His inspiring verses give voice to so much of the essence of Generative Change.

We send special thanks to Susanne Kessler who proofread these pages and beautifully embodied the role of a constructive critic.

We are particularly grateful to our illustrator Antonio Meza who did the amazing artwork for this book. Antonio's drawings truly represent the spirit of Generative Change and bring the book alive in ways that our words could not possibly accomplish.

Generative Coaching

Chapter 1

Overview of Generative Change

Background and Beginnings

The seeds of what we are calling "Generative Change" were planted over 40 years ago when the two of us met at the University of California at Santa Cruz in the mid-1970s. We were both students of John Grinder and Richard Bandler, the co-founders of NLP. We were also students of Gregory Bateson, who was a professor at UCSC at that time, and of Milton Erickson, the world-renowned hypnotherapist. These teachers were important influences on both of us and on the foundations of our Generative Change work.

One of the other things that we share is that we are both half Irish. Gilligan has the father half. Dilts has the mother half, which was Garigan. So it's Garigan and Gilligan. We like to say, with an Irish twinkle in our eyes, that Generative Change has an Irish father and an Irish mother.

And we also both went to all-boys Catholic high schools in the San Francisco Bay area in the late 1960s and early 1970s. All of this was a very generative time socially.

So, we share many things and are also very different in many ways. Our paths diverged for a while after our days at UC Santa Cruz. Professionally, Robert went on to become one of the main developers and trainers in the field of NLP. His NLP University in Santa Cruz is one of the most well-known and respected NLP training institutions. Steve became a major figure in the field of Ericksonian hypnosis and developed his own body of work known as Self-Relations.

After traveling our separate professional paths for some 25 years, we reconnected on a professional level in 1994 and began doing programs together that explored areas of common interest and integrated our complementary developments and styles. One of our first joint ventures was a program titled Love in the Face of Violence. Others included Genius and the Generative Self, The Evolution of Consciousness and The Hero's Journey, which became the basis for the book we co-authored on that topic entitled *The Hero's Journey: A Voyage of Self-Discovery* (2009).

As a result of these frequent generative collaborations, our complementary approaches became more integrated and a new, common body of work emerged that we call Generative Change.

The Three Branches of Generative Change

In this chapter, we will present a framework that defines what we mean by "Generative Change." *Generative Change* is a larger area of change work that contains the three different tracks of 1) Generative Trance, 2) Generative Coaching and 3) Generative Change in Business. Generative Trance is the result of the work that Stephen has done over the last 40 years, integrating Ericksonian hypnosis with his own innovations. Generative Change in Business is based on Robert's Success Factor Modeling work and his developments in NLP over the last 40 years and has to do with application of Generative Change to entrepreneurs, companies, organizations and leadership.

Generative Coaching is the fruit of our mutual collaboration, particularly over the last 15 + years. It involves applying the principles of Generative Change to the area of personal development through Life Coaching and Executive Coaching.

The principles and processes of Generative Change provide a "deep structure" that has many different applications. This deep structure of Generative Change can be applied to many diverse "surface structures" or issues and situations relating to individual, organizational and social change.

We are going to start with an overview of the Generative Change model and then, in the coming chapters, go into how we apply it specifically to coaching and the Six-Step Generative Coaching process that we have developed.

1. Generative Coaching

2. Generative Trance

**The Three Branches of
Generative Change**

3. Generative Change in Business

+ Community support and practice

For a New Beginning

Before diving into that, we both like to begin whatever we are presenting with a poem. We do this partly to honor our Irish roots, but also partly to emphasize that, in creativity, we're using language poetically and musically at least as much as literally. That is, we are looking to use language to open a space that includes yet transcends words at the same time.

The great writer Emerson used to say that, in fact, every word was a "fossil poem." That means each word has a history in it. Since we are not the first ones to speak them, the words we use carry clues about their origins and their evolution through time, like a fossil. But each word is also a poem, in that no word is really ultimately literal. It always has other layers of meaning.

The poem we would like to begin with is by an Irish writer named John O'Donohue. O'Donohue was probably best known for his book *Anam Cara*, which is the Gaelic term for "friend of the soul." But he wrote other things as well, and this is from a book of blessings that he wrote called "*Benedictus*." The poem is aptly titled *For a New Beginning*

For a New Beginning

In out-of-the-way places of the heart,
Where your thoughts never think to wander,
This beginning has been quietly forming,
Waiting until you were ready to emerge.
For a long time it has watched your desire,
Feeling the emptiness growing inside you,
Noticing how you willed yourself on,
Still unable to leave what you had outgrown.
It watched you play with the seduction of safety
And the gray promises that sameness whispered,
Heard the waves of turmoil rise and relent,
Wondered would you always live like this.
Then the delight, when your courage kindled,
And out you stepped onto new ground,
Your eyes young again with energy and dream,
A path of plenitude opening before you.
Though your destination is not yet clear
You can trust the promise of this opening;
Unfurl yourself into the grace of beginning
That is at one with your life's desire.
Awaken your spirit to adventure;
Hold nothing back, learn to find ease in risk;
Soon you will be home in a new rhythm,
For your soul senses the world that awaits you.

John O'Donohue

This poem captures a lot about the journey, challenges and joys of Generative Change – the often unconscious processes that trigger it, the struggle between the desire for familiarity and safety with the desire for growth, the energy and expansion that goes with connecting to your deepest passion and motivation, and the excitement of bringing something new into existence.

What is Generative Change and Why is it Important?

If there is one word that you could use to describe what Generative Change is about, it is *creativity*. When we grew up in the San Francisco Bay Area in the 60's, we thought it was all about *love*. However, now we believe that creativity is even more important than love, because creativity is not something that just a few special people do, but it is the heart and soul of everything we know as reality in the world. Modern neuroscience has established that anything that we humans know, we create. And so it brings up the question, "What is it that we want to create?" Generative Change work provides support for how to answer that question and implement our answers in a mindful and wise manner.

Generativity is actually a special type of creativity. Many types of creativity essentially involve reorganizing or incrementally improving something that already exists. Generativity is creativity in which you are making something completely new that has not existed before; i.e., "stepping out onto new ground" and where "your destination is not yet clear" as the poem describes.

There are times in the life of every system, every individual, every marriage, every family, every culture, every business, where what you have done in the past will not help you to go forward into the future. This is not everyday. Most of the time, you can use versions of what has worked in the past. However, where those of us who are change practitioners – coaches, consultants, therapists – come into people's lives is often where what they've done in the past can't help them in the present nor to achieve what they want for their future.

People sometimes use the metaphor of "rearranging the deck chairs on the Titanic" as a way of referring to the ineffectiveness of superficial change when you are in big trouble. Repositioning the chairs is not going to save the boat from running into an iceberg and sinking. You've got to go into a deeper place and make a more substantial change.

In this sense, generativity is about profound change. It's about deep structure change. You can have superficial creativity that just rearranges what you already know but, for us, generative change is about deep change that it is actually a change in the foundation of not only what you're doing, but in where you are trying to go.

Again, you can look at this in an individual, in small systems, or in big systems. We think most of us would agree that the major systems of the world today need some type of generative change. We're not talking about "boutique" changes or things that would be nice to add onto what we are already doing, but things that are crucial, particularly for the fundamental growth and survival of a system.

Conditions requiring generative change may include rapid growth into some new area, or a crisis where it is absolutely clear that what has worked before is no longer going to work and take you to the next stage. Or transition where you are really in between a very deep change in which you are no longer where you used to be, you're not yet where you're going to be, and you have to deal with a lot of uncertainty, a lot of risk, and a lot of potential danger. So, these are some examples of the times when we need generative change.

Key Elements of Generative Change Work

There are a number of key elements of Generative Change work. These include:

* The importance of a generative state
* Going somewhere completely new – Goals are expressed as a positive intention: i.e. Direction versus Destination
* The generative relationship: A field of conversation in which $1 + 1 = 3$ or more
* The importance of aesthetic intelligence
* The approach to dealing with "negative" influences (Aikido) – Creative nonviolence
* Practice as a foundation for conscious living

The first point we will be emphasizing is that Generative Change of any type requires that the individual, group or system be in a *generative state*. We will be going into what we mean by that in more depth later in this chapter.

The second key point has to do with *establishing goals in the form of an intention*, as opposed to a clearly defined objective. Often, when you are in times of uncertainty, you cannot know the ultimate destination. You cannot know the specifics of your final goal. You only know "I have to go in that direction. The desired state is that way."

This is partly because there is no single map that will adequately describe the situation or provide the solution. So, in order to generate something new, you need to work with multiple contradictory maps simultaneously.

Generative change requires that the system is in a generative state.

Establishing goals in the form of an intention.

This also brings us to the notion of what we call a *generative relationship*. The foundation of all Generative Change work is that "one plus one does not always make two." In the right conditions, it could also make three, four, five or more. That is, in fact, the implication of "generative." The interaction generates something beyond the elements involved in the interaction.

And to establish a generative relationship, we need to be attuned to our own individual positions and points of view, yet we also need equally to be able to be attuned to the position and perspective of the others we are interacting with. And what we are looking for are the differences, looking for where the other person's consciousness has a different map or point of view than my consciousness. In fact, that's how we make babies – "A little bit of this and a little bit of that."

This is where the importance of *aesthetic intelligence* comes in. As you are working to identify and integrate those differences, too much of one begins to become a problem. It creates imbalance and disharmony. So, we're looking for that harmonious bringing together of "a little bit of one and a little bit of another." When we keep interacting and combining this way that's what makes a beautiful image or beautiful music.

Some simple examples of aesthetic relationships would be a superb meal, a musical orchestra, a great story, a successful sports team, a high performing business team, a creative person, a functional family, culture or community. In each case, you have differences, but the differences complement each other in a way where they work together harmoniously and beautifully.

In a generative relationship, you are constantly shifting with respect to one another to produce something pleasurable without needing to get rid of any part of yourself. In doing so, you find that you have expanded yourself in ways that you didn't imagine as possible before the relationship.

You are growing through the relationship. The differences add and expand. It's not, "Okay I'll give up this and you give up that. And then we can do something." We are fully committed to our perspective, but we can include other perspectives and expand our view of what is possible. That is where you really get something that's ultimately new and unpredictable.

Dealing Generatively with Obstacles and Interferences

The other key dynamic in Generative Change is *how we deal with potentially negative interferences*, which often come from differences. One person (or part of a person) wants to go "this" way, the other person (or part) wants to go "that" way. Now this could easily become a problem, so we need to hold those differences in a creative field, in a creative environment that allows all of the parties to be able to appreciate what they can bring that is beyond any one of them individually.

Another way of saying this is that what we are trying to do in generative change is to create a space where each piece of the change process – the present state, the desired state, the resources and the obstacles – all are given a place.

This positive relationship to obstacles as an integral part of any meaningful change is something we will be focusing on continuously because we think it's one of the unique contributions that Generative Change makes to fields of therapy, coaching and consulting.

This approach to obstacles didn't originate with us. Our common teacher Milton Erickson was just astonishing in his ability to welcome these strange, disturbing patterns and then be able to engage with them in a way that they become a resource in front of our very eyes.

Steve practiced the Japanese martial arts Aikido for 16 years and experienced time and again the same exploration of, if you're given this disturbing and seemingly negative energy, how do you relationally engage with it? Our fight-or-flight automatic reaction usually creates more aggression. It creates more hatred and more negativity. So, in generative change we are exploring what happens if both polarities can stay grounded and "make babies" together.

One of the basic principles of generative change is that "Any particular response is actually neither good nor bad, dangerous or not dangerous. What will make it one way or the other is how one responds to it, which could be thousands of ways." So, that's part of what generativity is about. How can I shift my relationship with what is there in order to bring out something different, something better or something new?

Ultimately, this experience gets created out of the relational connection between the parties or parts of the system involved. In practices like Aikido, the question becomes, "When I meet this difficult energy that way, how do I feel about myself, how do I feel about the other person, and how do I feel about us?"

In generative change we hold our differences in a creative field to discover and appreciate our generative complementarities.

In generative change, we view any particular response as only one of the many possible expressions of a more fundamental deep structure. And it is how we meet and interact with that response that determines which one of those many possible expressions is the one that actually emerges or comes out.

Creativity as the Interaction Between the "Quantum Field" and the "Classical World"

One way to talk about that would be in terms of the dynamic between the "quantum world" and the "classical world" in physics. The quantum world is essentially a field of infinite possibilities – all of the possible forms something could take. The classical world is made up of one particular ongoing, concrete expression of all of those possibilities. The quantum field holds infinite possibilities. The classical world chooses one reality.

In any creative process, we typically start in this non-classical, non-physical quantum field. To give some examples of what a quantum field might look like, consider Monet's paintings or look at how they make functional MRIs. MRIs are the brain images where they take multiple images from different perspectives and drop them into a space together where you have maybe 25 different images. From these, they create some sort of deep structure or archetype that represents the deeper pattern.

What this means practically would be, if Robert is being aggressive and Steve's response is, "Well he's a f***ing angry ba****rd," Robert's aggression will likely escalate and emerge in a fairly violent form. And Steve would say, "We've got to get him on medication," or "We've got to get him on anger control." He'd be thinking that this pattern is just negative anger.

What we're looking to do in generative change is create this working space, where we can see that infinite possibilities are in every expression. To do that, we need to move from the classical world, where the quantum wave has collapsed to one specific expression, back into the "ocean of infinite possibility." So, we realize inside of that anger is the potential for so many different forms of concrete expression.

This is what we mean by a generative state, which can be achieved through a variety of ways. Shamanism, mindfulness, self-hypnosis, state management, etc., are all modalities that help us to start to bring some particular expression back into a space of many possible forms. And this is where the aesthetic intelligence comes in. When in this state of many possibilities, I can re-engage the response and help shape it into a form that is much more harmonious, and that actually even serves the positive purpose of that response even better.

Anger, for instance, may have the positive intention of setting a boundary, protecting something or taking decisive action. Rather than coming out as shouting or physical violence, the same intention and energy could express as taking a committed stand, taking a heroic action or making a peaceful protest.

We can summarize this dynamic in the following way:

Premise 1 : Creativity is a conversation

1. This conversation is between the creative unconscious (*quantum*) and the conscious (*classical*) worlds.

2. The creative unconscious is a holographic wave field containing "infinite possibilities".

3. The conscious mind "collapses the quantum wave" to create one reality.

4. Creativity moves between these two worlds, each completes the other.

One of the main functions of a generative state is to move from a place where there is only one meaning and one possibility to a place where whatever is happening is resonating and vibrating and we can see it has many different possible expressions and meanings. That is the first step in our creative process – entering this open state where we can welcome something not as a fixed, negative thing that has to be fought with or suppressed, but rather as a pattern that has so much potential to be so many different things, if we can just create the proper conditions for welcoming it.

As an illustration, you can think of a newborn child as an individual in a quantum state because there are so many possibilities yet to be expressed. In the view of NLP, the baby starts to develop certain "neuro-linguistic programs," through their interactions with family members, friends, teachers, media exposure, etc., that start to filter out certain possibilities and accentuate others. So, as we become programmed by our families, education, culture and media, instead of having all the possibilities that we could have, we have a smaller, more limited range.

A good example of this phenomenon is the study that was done by people who simply were looking at the number of movements that a person would make in an hour. They reported that if you observe a six months old child for one hour and you watch what they do, you'll see something like a thousand different movements – with their head, with their arms, legs, fingers, face, etc.

But if you take the same child when they're 10 years old and you watch them for an hour, you won't see a thousand discreet movements anymore. You will be lucky to see a few hundred. Of course, the child has gotten more efficient. They've become more structured in what they do. They are more effective in some ways. But they have also lost a fair amount of flexibility.

If you take the same person at 30 years old, you might be lucky to see even a hundred different movements. So, we start to limit those quantum possibilities. On the one hand, this allows us to perform things more easily and efficiently, but in these times of change that we were talking about, in these times of crisis, in these times of growth, in these times of transition, those familiar patterns no longer serve us. And if we cannot get back to that quantum state of many possibilities, then we become increasingly limited. We get caught in rigidity.

Creativity is a Function of the State of Our Filters

In our generative change work, we talk about three general types of filters. This is finally an application of the mystery of the "Holy Trinity" that we both grew up with as part of our Catholic education. Steve got kicked out of Jesuit High School for challenging the mystery of the Trinity. So, it's great to have a practical application "In the name of the cognitive, and the somatic and the holy field, amen."

But, seriously, we are saying that the "light" of the "quantum ocean of possibilities" is coming through these filters. The manner in which those filters are set projects the reality that we perceive and respond to. Steve did his graduate work in Psychology at Stanford University in Palo Alto, and did about 30 experiments over five years on what's called "state-dependent learning and memory." Steve would hypnotically train people to get into certain emotional states, such as sadness, anger, or happiness, and then look at how that emotional state influenced a variety of different cognitive processes such as remembering experiences from childhood.

He found that when people are in a sad state, they would remember a preponderance of sad memories. But if you took that same person and shifted them into a happy state, their childhood memories were qualitatively different. The kind of future that they would imagine from a sad state versus a happy state was qualitatively different. What they would notice out in the world and the interpretations that they would make about what they noticed were different.

This is an example of the profound influence of perceptual filters. Psychology is basically the study of such filters. Generative change is about how to apply such filters to create new possibilities.

A good symbol for the influence of filtering is a prism. If you put white light through a prism it divides the "quantum potential" of the white light into distinct, separate colors. You can put different kinds of filters on the white light such that only certain colors show up. If you are not aware of the filter, you end up thinking that the whole world is that way.

As an analogy, if the filter only passes the blue light spectrum, all we see is blue (say, sadness). Perhaps the filter is set to pass only red (e.g., anger). Then we only perceive what irritates us and angers us.

So, in our generative change work, we say it all begins with the state of our filters.

We can summarize the influence of our filters in the following way:

Premise 2 : Reality construction occurs via filters

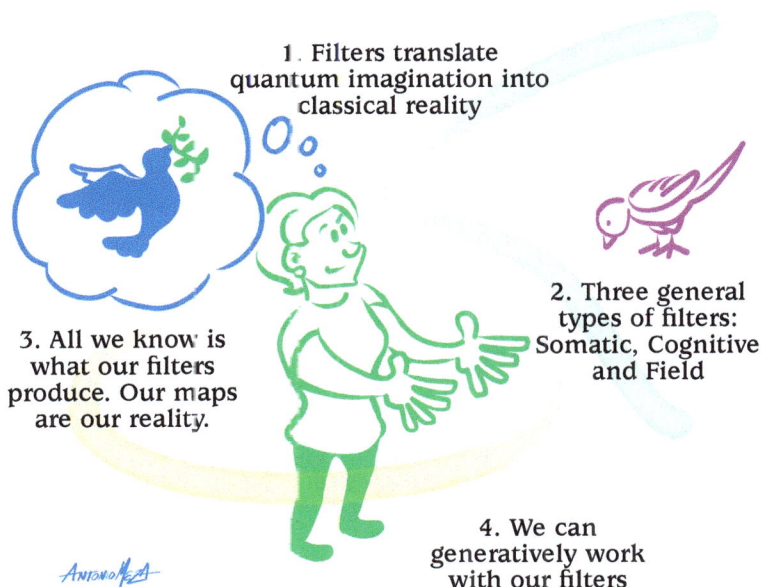

1. Filters translate quantum imagination into classical reality

2. Three general types of filters: Somatic, Cognitive and Field

3. All we know is what our filters produce. Our maps are our reality.

4. We can generatively work with our filters

CRASH Versus COACH: The State of our Filters is Determined by Our Degree of Presence and Mindfulness

What determines the state of the filters is the quality of human presence that is holding those filters. You can be holding them in really tight, mindless way or you can be holding them in a state of creative flow.

So, the point is that you are holding one set of filters within another, more fundamental set of filters. This is the notion of what we call COACH versus CRASH. When my cognitive and somatic filters are held from a mindful, open state, I will perceive many possibilities. If the same filters are held within a mindless, reactive state, I will perceive very few alternatives.

We call this mindless, reactive state of our filters "CRASH." **C**ontracted; **R**eactive; **A**nalysis, paralysis; **S**eparated and isolated, and feeling **H**ostile, hurt and hurtful. How many of you have ever experienced a state like that? Most of the time when people are stuck in problems, this is the main culprit.

Another term for a CRASH state is "neuromuscular lock." In such a state, the only possible responses we perceive available to us are fundamental survival strategies, such as attacking (fight), running away from (flight), spacing out (freeze), or collapsing (fold).

As an analogy, if you set the optical filter to only filter for the blue spectrum, and you're asking it to find red, it's never going to find it. The state of your filters is going to determine what is possible for you to perceive, and what you perceive is possible.

Let us repeat that. The state of your filters is going to determine what is possible for you. So, if you keep getting the same unwanted result in some area of your life, that is telling you something about the state of your filters. The universe itself is changing in every moment. So it is the state of your filters that is creating the same unwanted reality over and over and over. It's your filters that you need to look at.

To do that, you have to really tune in mindfully to the space in which you're holding your thoughts, your awareness of your body and your awareness of your relationships. We do that through what we call the COACH state: **C**entered in your body, **O**pen in mind and heart, **A**ware and awake to yourself and the others around you, **C**onnected to your resources and to others, and **H**olding what is happening from a state of hospitality, curiosity and resourcefulness.

Premise 3 : Filters are held by human consciousness: "Mindless of Mindful"

CRASH state

COACH state

When held mindlessly with neuromuscular lock - *fight, flight, freeze or fold* – problems develop and repeat themselves.

When held mindfully with *creative flow*, solutions and new learnings are possible.

Contracted

Reactive

Analysis Paralysis

Separated

Hostile / Hurting / Hating

Centered

Open

Aware

Connected

Holding

Nelson Mandela is a beautiful example of someone who was able to live from a sustained COACH state and the potential for change that creates. Just imagine what he went through. Thirty-plus years in prison, torture, and seeing his people endure extreme hardship. Do you think you could look like the person in this photo after all that? So, what was he doing that allowed him to regain and sustain this positive state in such challenging conditions? That's one of our practical questions.

Centering in our body is the first key. Getting down, underneath your verbal, cognitive mind. It helps you to connect with something deeper than your mental programming and the limited state of your filters. You center beneath them.

Centered

Then we can *open beyond* them. The **O** of COACH state is about opening your mind and opening your heart to a bigger space of possibilities. What is important, however, is to open out from your center.

Open

The **A** is about awareness. To stay present and mindful, we need more and more nuanced awareness and greater self-awareness. Very often, we're not aware of the state of our own filters, especially when we are in a CRASH state. It takes great practice. This is one of the reasons we need a coach at times – to give us feedback about the state of our filters so that we can become more conscious and able to choose to adjust them if necessary.

Aware

The second **C** of the COACH state is about our level of connection to ourselves – head, heart, belly, body, emotions, intellect, etc., – our connection to others and to the resources outside of ourselves. Any place we are disconnected, we are "off-line."

The **H** of COACH refers to the capacity to "hold" whatever is happening and what we are experiencing with curiosity, resourcefulness and a welcoming mindset. One way to illustrate and understand what we mean by "holding" is the following diagram of a little circle inside of a larger circle.

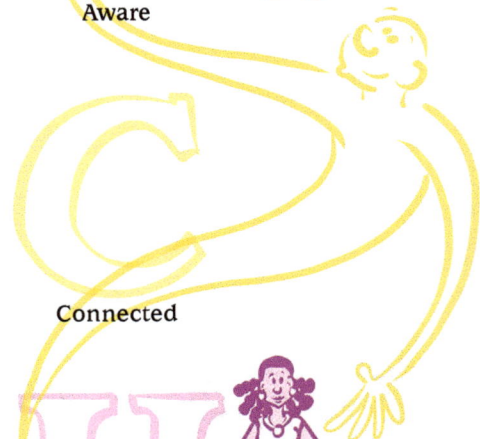

Connected

Holding

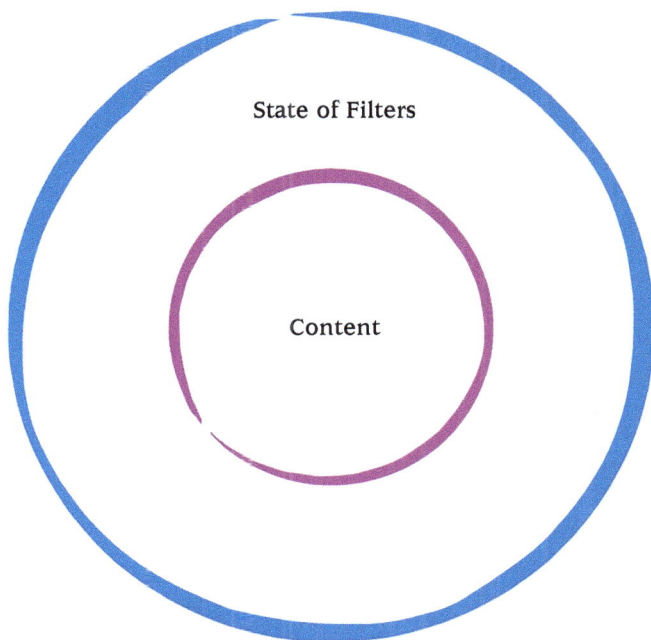

State of Filters

Content

The larger circle represents the state of the filters within which the content is being perceived and acted upon. The way in which the content is held will determine our relationship with that content and the way in which that content is perceived and expressed. When a particular content is held in a CRASH state it is likely to be perceived and expressed as something difficult, dangerous and problematic. If the same content is held within the filters of the COACH state, it is more likely to be perceived and expressed in a productive and resourceful way.

This is one of our most fundamental premises of Generative Change: Any particular content (i.e., emotion, behavior, symptom, relationship, situation, etc.) can be positive or negative, helpful or unhelpful, good or bad, useful or problematic depending upon the state of your filters and the relationship you have with that content. If I treat something as a problem, it will be a problem. If I treat the same thing as an opportunity, it will be an opportunity.

It is interesting to note that Robert and his wife Deborah first came up with the acronyms for COACH and CRASH one morning in 2009 when they were working through a particularly difficult dynamic in their relationship. The acronyms helped them to both keep remembering to come back to a resourceful state when things got especially challenging. (And they are still practicing today.)

The Basic Steps of Generative Change

So, a key practical question becomes "How can I keep my filters in a generative COACH state, regardless of what is happening?" Learning the answer to this question is an essential part of all three tracks of Generative Change – Generative Trance, Generative Coaching and Generative Consulting. They all share a common deep structure, and a common path of steps. This deep structure can be adapted to many different contents.

1. The first step involves "emptying out" or *"clearing the channel."* Creativity research shows that an important part of the creative process is frequently to take a rest, go for a walk and take your mind off the problem. It is usually during this period that some new idea comes. There is consensus among the creativity researchers that what's happening there is you are releasing all of your wrong answers. It is a process of letting go in order to let something new come in.

So if you are going to engage in any type of generative change work, the first thing you want to do, before starting to talk about the problem or about the desired state or the potential solution, is to open your filters, clear your channel and connect to the best of yourself and to what we've been calling the "quantum field" of infinite possibilities. Simply put, you want to empty out, open the channel and "clear the mechanism." This essentially means getting everyone involved into a COACH state. That's always step one.

1. Clearing the channel

2. Setting a positive intention

3. Entering a generative performance state

2. Next you want to direct that connection to yourself, each other and that field of infinite possibilities toward some purpose –; what we call a *"positive intention."* We are asking the question, "What's the future that is waiting to be created through you?" And, as we have pointed out, in generative change we can't know what the final concrete expression of that intention is going to be when we start. The important thing is to be clear about the direction, even if we do not know precisely what the destination will be like.

3. Once you have your filters open and directed toward a positive intention, the third step is to enter what we call a *generative performance state.* To do this, you are answering the question "What would be my best performance state to be able to move in the world to make this intention real?

The difference between the COACH state and what we're calling the "generative performance state" is that, in addition to the connection to yourself and your center, you are adding a second connection to a particular direction or "intention." To complete the generative state, you add a third connection to specific parts of your larger "field of resources." This can include what you have learned or received from teachers, mentors, family, ancestors, nature, etc. So, the purpose of the generative state is to direct, open and adjust my filters in order to be able to bring my positive intention into concrete expression.

In generative change work, these first three steps are the precursors to moving into action – to answering the question, "What do I do?" Usually when people come to you for consulting, for coaching or for therapy, they're desperately asking, "What do I do? What do I do? What do I do? What do I do?" And usually your first response is to immediately ask yourself, "What do I do? What do I do? What do I do? What I do? What do I do?" And our sincere response is "nothing," at least at first. Before taking action, you've got to empty out and get clear about what direction your client really wants to go. Then you have to organize yourself and whoever else is involved to be in a creative state.

4. After that, you can move to the fourth step of the generative change process, which is *exploring how we're going to get from the present state to the desired state.* The research on creativity and "flow" shows clearly that you've got to work in small chunks. If you have just one big goal, it's too much, too vague, too overwhelming, and it's not going to happen. You've got to chunk it down and organize it on a timeline. So, we're thinking "What would be the concrete steps to take to reach that intention?"

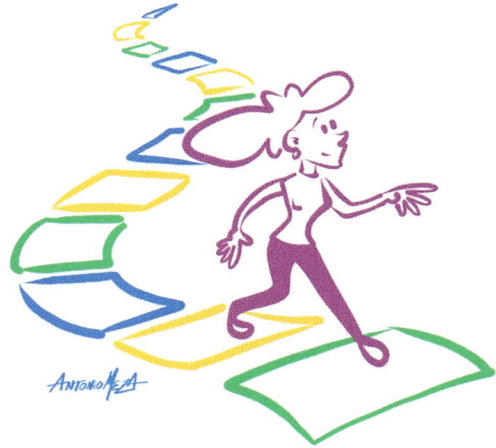

4. Chunking down the path

5. It is about this time (although it really could come just about anywhere in the process) that step five happens, whether you want it to or not. *You begin to confront the inevitable external and internal obstacles.* As soon as you think, "Okay, I'm going to go for that intention with confidence," what almost immediately gets activated are all of those inner and outer presences that say, "Oh no, you're not." "You're stupid." "You're crazy." "You can't do it." "Who do you think you are anyway?" "Do you have a license for that?" "It's going to cost you too much money."

5. Transforming obstacles

As we have pointed out, this is one of the most important parts of generative change. Usually, within five seconds of a person stating a goal, you can you can see the inner obstacles activate. Within five seconds of when the person says, "This is what I want" something inside says, "No, you can't have it."

This is an expression of one of our most fundamental principles of generative change work, which is that "everything contains its opposite." As soon as I say I want more happiness, the opposite will start to emerge. All the experiences and places of sadness and grief begin to show up. Isaac Newton claimed that "for every action, there's an equal and opposite reaction." And the same thing is true psychologically. For every goal, there are going to be equal and opposite obstacles. We like to say "the brighter the light, the darker the shadow." The bigger the goal, the bigger are the "demons" that will come to stop you.

The most important thing to do when the obstacles come is to remain in the COACH state and generative state. The natural reaction is to begin to enter some form of CRASH (attack, run away, freeze or give up). Remaining in a resourceful, generative state requires training and practice. One of the main things that Steve practiced in his Aikido training for over 16 years was, as soon as you feel somebody grab you, you relax and take their energy through you into the earth. That allows you to have a curious skillful COACH relationship to what just entered the system. If you fall into a sustained CRASH state at that point, the system is going to CRASH too.

This is where keeping the connection to the field of quantum possibility comes in. This obstacle is coming in a certain form. If we can meet it, hold it (the "H" part of COACH) and bring it into a "shimmering" state of possibilities, then we can actually begin to transform its expression. That's the notion of "transforming the obstacle." What appears to be an obstacle or interference takes a different form that actually can become in some ways a guardian or a guide.

6. As we have pointed out, doing all of this requires practice. So, the sixth step of the generative change process involves *estab-lishing ongoing practices* that will sustain your momentum toward reaching your intention and deepen the change you are striving to make. Practices are repetitive activities that strengthen and enrich your progress to achieving your positive intention.

6. Establishing ongoing practices

In the coming chapters, we will be exploring how we apply the principles and process of generative change specifically to coaching.

We Are Messengers

We may leave our footprints
on the earth,
but we walk in heaven.
Our light shines beyond
our own vision,
our words sink deeper
than our own wisdom

We teach
what we have lived before
does not determine
what we can become

And we follow
a simple truth
of the heart:

What we see in others
we awaken in ourselves

We become
what we give
to the world.

– Nick LeForce

Chapter 2

Introduction to Generative Coaching

In the previous chapter, we laid the foundation of the deep structure of all generative change work. In this chapter we are going to provide an overview of how we apply that deep structure to the process of coaching. While Generative Trance, Generative Coaching and Generative Change in Business all share the same basic prototype, there are differences in the ways that deep structure is applied and where you focus your attention.

Let's start by taking a look at how what we call "coaching" developed.

History of Coaching

In general, coaching is the process of helping people and teams to perform at the peak of their abilities. It involves drawing out people's strengths, helping them to bypass personal barriers and limits in order to achieve their personal best, and facilitating them to function more effectively as members of a team. Thus, effective coaching requires an emphasis on both task and relationship.

Traditional coaching concentrates on defining and achieving specific goals. Coaching methodologies are outcome-oriented rather than problem-oriented. They tend to be highly solution-focused, promoting the development of effective strategies for thinking and acting as opposed to trying to resolve problems and past conflicts. Problem solving, or remedial change, is more associated with counseling and therapy.

Interestingly, the term "coach" comes from the name of a small Hungarian village, *Kocs*, where superior wagons, carts and carriages were built in the 16th and 17th centuries. Kocs lay on the main road along the Danube between Vienna and Budapest. These two great cities needed well-built, fast vehicles that would carry more than two people over the bumpy roads of the day in as much comfort as possible. One of the best of these multi-horse carts – a light, reasonably comfortable four-wheeled passenger wagon with a strap suspension – was called in Hungarian *kocsi szekér*, literally "a wagon from Kocs." It was so compact, elegant and sturdy that the design spread throughout Europe. The Viennese called the vehicle a *Kutsche* after the Hungarian town. In Paris, the French adapted the Austrian word to coche. In Rome it became cocchio. Eventually, the vehicle showed up in England and was called a *coach*.

Thus, a coach originally meant "a wagon or carriage" and still carries this meaning today—such as when a person travels "coach" on a railway or airline. A "coach" is literally *a vehicle that carries a person or group of people from some starting location to a desired location.*

As an example, we both frequently take the Eurostar train to travel between Paris and London. The last time we took the train, they assigned us seats for "Coach 13." We were thinking "Oh, boy! We're going to get coached the whole way there!" But, of course, it wasn't referring to a person. Literally, the coach in this sense meant a particular part of the vehicle that was taking us from one place to another.

A "Coach" is a Vehicle that Transports People From Some Present State to a Desired State

The Development of Traditional Coaching

The notion of coaching in the educational sense derived from the concept that the tutor "conveys" or "transports" the student through his or her examinations. An educational coach is defined as "a private tutor," "one who instructs or trains a performer or a team of performers," or "one who instructs players in the fundamentals of a competitive sport and directs team strategy." The process of being a coach is defined as "to train intensively (as by instruction and demonstration)."

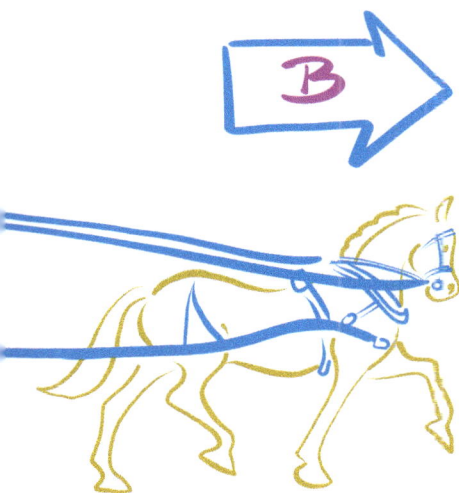

In sports, the coach accompanies and observes the athletes while they practice, providing encouragement and feedback for them to give their best performance. A rowing coach, for instance, rides in a boat that moves along next to the rowers. The coach observes the rowers and directs their attention to various aspects of their performance both individually and as a team, saying things like, "Watch the knees of the person in front of you"; "Open your chest and keep your shoulders strong and soft."

So, in a sense, the coach relationship is the vehicle that transports the client to the desired state. And a great deal of the attention is put on taking action. Sports coaching, voice coaching, acting coaching, etc., are all directed towards specific types of behavioral activities. A voice coach helps you to improve your voice. A batting coach helps improve your ability to hit a baseball. And so on.

Coaching, then, is about supplying a vehicle by which a person or a group can move from their *present state* to some *desired state* along, hopefully, the most efficient and effective *path*. To accomplish this journey, key resources must be identified and put into place and potential *interferences* must also be identified and appropriately dealt with. We can summarize the basic coaching process in the following diagram.

Rowing coach

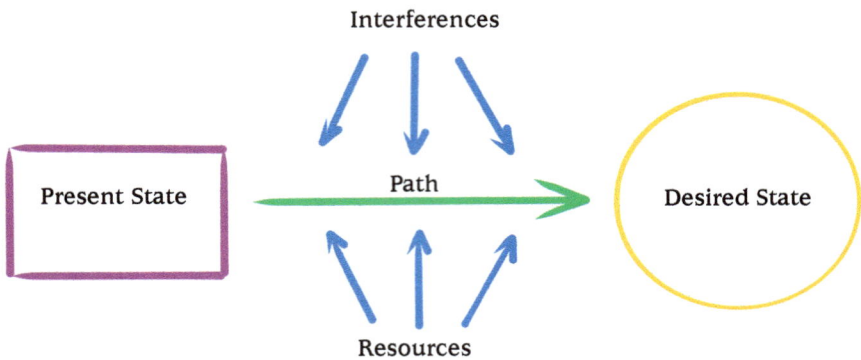

Interferences

Present State — Path → Desired State

Resources

Diagram of the General Coaching Process

Large "C" and Small "c" Coaching

Historically, coaching has typically been focused toward achieving improvement with respect to a specific behavioral performance. An effective coach of this type (such as a "voice coach," an "acting coach," a "pitching coach") observes a person's behavior and gives him or her tips and guidance about how to improve in specific contexts and situations. This involves promoting the development of that person's behavioral competence through careful observation and feedback.

Coaching that promotes generative change, however, needs to provide support on a number of different levels: behaviors, capabilities, beliefs, values and even identity. We refer to this type of coaching as capital "C" Coaching (see *From Coach to Awakener*, R. Dilts, 2003).

Small "c" coaching is more focused at a behavioral level, referring to the process of helping another person to achieve or improve a particular behavioral performance. Small "c" coaching methods derive primarily from a sports training model, promoting conscious awareness of resources and abilities, and the development of conscious competence.

Large "C" Coaching or Generative Coaching, involves helping people to effectively achieve outcomes on a range of levels. It emphasizes generative change, concentrating on strengthening identity and values, and bringing dreams and goals into reality. This encompasses the skills of small "c" coaching, but also includes much more.

So, we can say that Generative Coaching is a form of Large "C" coaching. Instead of focusing on a specific category of behavior, we are bringing on our focus to "What is it that you most want to create in your life?" And then "How are you going to create that?" Again, it is that movement of bringing something from the quantum field of possibilities into concrete action.

In fact, for us, Generative Coaching is leading the way to a new generation of change work.

The Three Generations of Personal Change Work

If we look at the history of personal development and change work, we can say that the first generation was traditional therapy. When we (Robert and Stephen) were first involved in developing NLP in the mid-1970s, there were no formal fields of Life Coaching or Executive Coaching. If you wanted to get involved in the field of personal development, you essentially had to do it by learning some form of therapy. And that traditionally meant somebody did something to somebody else who couldn't do it for themselves, or who had a problem or was broken. The therapist had the answer and the tools – the client was essentially just a receiver.

To be fair, there had begun in the 1950's a sort of a shift-away from this type of therapy with people like Carl Rogers or Jean Houston in humanistic psychology, or Virginia Satir and Milton Erickson in more systemic approaches to therapy. There was also everything that was happening California in the 60's. Esalen, for instance, which is just an hour and a half down the coast from Santa Cruz, is where they did California encounter therapy in hot tubs.

So there had been this movement in terms of non-pathological ways of supporting people's growth and development. But it was a little bit hodge-podge. And then in the 80's that began to constellate in this idea of "coaching." The movement involved a shift from an authoritarian, past orientation, problem-symptom orientation to a collaborative, future-focused, solution orientation. This started with the development of things like solution-focused therapy. Then, in coaching, the focus shifted even further from finding solutions to reaching desired outcomes. Problems are not intended to be the focus at all. The questions are, "Where do you want to go?" and "What are the steps to get there?"

One of the limitations of the traditional coaching approach, however, is that it tends to be too much social-cognitive-verbal-left brain. The focus is almost entirely on what we are calling the "classical world." So, we would call traditional coaching "The first generation of coaching." It's a little bit too much up in the head. It doesn't want to deal with problems. And it is not very embodied. The approach is essentially, "Just focus on what you want. Quit complaining. Find your resources, go and do it."

So, in this second generation of change work, there was a shift from "The therapist has the solution, the client is helpless" in the first generation therapy; to "The coach doesn't have the answer, the client has the answer" as a basic tenet of coaching. The role of the coach is to support the client to find his or her own answers and solutions.

In the third generation of change work, characterized by generative coaching, we say, "It's not Either-Or, it's Both-And." The past and the problem and the future and the outcome are all part of the overall change process. The first of the core principles of generative change is that "creativity is a conversation." And, in our view, the creative mind is not in the coach, nor is it in the client. It is in the field between them. It is in the quality of the relationship. It's in the conversation. And so like musicians, you have to create the conditions to be listening and speaking in some sort of balanced way.

Secondly, the creative mind and the answers are not just in the head, not just in the conscious mind. Nor are they, as in the view of traditional hypnosis, just in the unconscious. The creative mind and the answers are in this conversational balance between the unconscious, quantum world and the conscious, classical world.

Thirdly, creativity and change are not just a function of solutions and resources. Rather, creativity and change involve solution and resources *plus* the problem and the obstacles at the same time. And that when you can hold these opposite energies simultaneously, something new begins to emerge. And that's what the word "generative" is intended to point to.

We can summarize this evolution in the following way.

1. **First generation change work:** Traditional Therapy – Authoritarian; oriented to past problems and pathology; verbally oriented, more talk than action.

2. **Second generation change work:** New Therapies/Traditional Coaching – Collaborative; oriented to future; solutions and resources; focused on action; creativity is in either the conscious OR unconscious.

3. **Third generation change work:** Generative Coaching (i.e., creating novel outcomes, deep change, transformational) – Emergent; traditional coaching *PLUS* engaging the creative consciousness; generative internal states; transforming problems into resources; oriented to creative consciousness in both inner and outer worlds, creating realities "beyond belief and expectation".

Third generation change work:
Generative Coaching

GO! DO IT!

Second generation change work:
Traditional Coaching

I'LL FIX YOU

BLAH...

First generation change work: Traditional Therapy

It is important to point out that we are not saying that any of these generations are "right" or "wrong" or better than the others. Each has its purpose, its focus and its function. As we have pointed out, this third generation of Generative Change work is necessary and most effective when the goal is to create something novel and new, especially in situations that involve a high level of change and uncertainty. These are situations where the old answers and solutions no longer work.

The Differences Between Generative Coaching, Generative Trance and Generative Change in Business

Speaking of the three tracks of generative change, we frequently get asked the question "What are the differences between Generative Trance, Generative Coaching and Generative Change in Business?" Since they obviously share a common deep structure, a lot of it has to do with the focus of how this deep structure is applied.

All generative change involves this type of dance between the inner (and more quantum) world and the outer (more classical) world, directed towards a particular desired state. As we have said, traditional coaching is focused on doing or improving something behavioral (i.e., voice, acting, gymnastics, etc.). This is what we are referring to when we talk about achieving something in the concrete, external, classical world. When we set an intention in generative coaching, we're typically looking to get something new moving more into the concrete world – e.g., write a book, grow my consulting practice, improve my intimate relationship, establish better eating habits, etc. People generally seek coaching in order to make some type of concrete self-improvement.

With generative trance, the focus of the intention is frequently more internal and personal, often involving some type of healing or inner transformation. Generative Coaching grounds things more in the classical world, Generative Trance tends to spend more time exploring the quantum world. The notion of "trance" is clearly associated with the "creative unconscious." To support a client to enter that space, a Generative Trance practitioner needs to be a bit more of a guide, taking the place of the client's conscious mind temporarily, and using certain types of suggestions so that the client can more fully enter their quantum imagination. This requires a unique set of skills distinct from those used in coaching.

A good illustration of this is the contrast between the Meta Model and the Milton Model in the development of NLP. When we first came together in the initial Bandler-Grinder groups, the first model that Bandler and Grinder came up with was called the "Meta Model." In their book *The Structure of Magic I*, Bandler and Grinder applied principles of transformational grammar to model the verbal skills of psychotherapeutic geniuses like Virginia Satir and Fritz Perls. The Meta Model basically maps out a system of questions these therapists used to help their clients get more consciously specific and aware of how the "deletions, distortions and generalizations" in their models of the world were limiting them. Some examples of these questions are, "What specifically? Who specifically? How specifically?" These are all about getting a more clear and specific map.

When Bandler and Grinder showed *The Structure of Magic I* to Gregory Bateson, he said, "If you guys really want to know something about communication, go study 'the purple one' out in the desert." (We like to point out that Milton Erickson was "the purple one" before Prince.) Bandler and Grinder went down to Phoenix, Arizona to model Erickson and came away completely confused, which was the common response in hanging out with Milton Erickson. And what they found was that Erickson was systematically violating every Meta Model distinction. He was doing the opposite of asking questions to get more consciously specific. As a hypnotherapist, he was more likely to make open-ended suggestions that propelled people more into the quantum field of the creative unconscious. And so, in *The Patterns of Milton Erickson Volume 1*, Bandler and Grinder basically had to invert the Meta Model to be called the "Milton Model." It was all about using unspecific language and metaphors.

So, Generative Trance is more about using the Milton Model. It is about taking a journey into the quantum field. In Generative Trance you're helping the client find some place that they are locked into and then using trance to unbind that place. We loosen all commitment to any particular perspective or understanding until we find multiple new possibilities, and then try those on for size.

Coaching is a bit more to the Meta Model side and getting specific by asking certain types of questions. How specifically will you do this? Let's chunk that down. However, even in Generative Coaching, you need to dip into that quantum state for a while in order to get something new and then come back in order to continue the journey.

So, part of what you are looking to do discern, as a generative change practitioner of any type, is when you need to be more open and when you need to be more precise – when you need to really get specific, and when you need to let go of the focus on a particular representation and open to a deeper structure where you have infinite possible forms.

This is where aesthetic intelligence comes in. Because if you get too focused on one part, you'll start to lose the connection to the other. In generative change we're always doing "both and." I'm going to the specific while at the same time I'm keeping connection to the whole. That's the aesthetic intelligence of it. To do this we need to keep the balance of "relaxed readiness" in the body and "focused spaciousness" in the mind. That's part of the power of the COACH state. "I'm focused and spacious simultaneously. I'm relaxed and ready simultaneously."

The movement from Generative Coaching to Generative Change in Business tends to lean even a bit more to the classical world and the bigger whole. The goal of *Generative Change in Business* is to help teams and organizations evolve and function in ways that are both new and more effective. Accomplishing this involves advising clients with respect to establishing a program or path that integrates multiple intelligences and multiple interventions in order to reach key organizational outcomes that have potentially never been achieved before. Even if a consultant is interacting with a single individual, the focus is not ultimately on that particular individual. That individual is perceived as a representative of a bigger system.

All generative change, of course, involves getting access to the quantum field. So, Generative Change in Business emphasizes the use of metaphor, the body and somatic intelligence to a much greater degree than traditional consulting which generally works exclusively with left-brain, rational constructs. Generative Consulting also draws heavily upon what we are calling the "field" mind in the form of collective intelligence.

In summary, we can say that both Generative Coaching and Generative Trance focus more on the individual. Generative Trance involves creating more access to the quantum field of the creative unconscious, using various forms of guidance and suggestion to produce inner healing and transformation. Generative Coaching tends to work to create self-improvement that is grounded more in the outer, classical world; though it still requires frequent and rich connections to the quantum field. Generative Change in Business focuses on achieving something new in the bigger systems that we are part of as individuals. Generative Change in Business is about applying the principles of generative change in order to offer advice for how to create a path for some new achievement in the outer, classical world. The ultimate goal of all three, however, is individual and collective empowerment. That is the "pattern that connects" all of them.

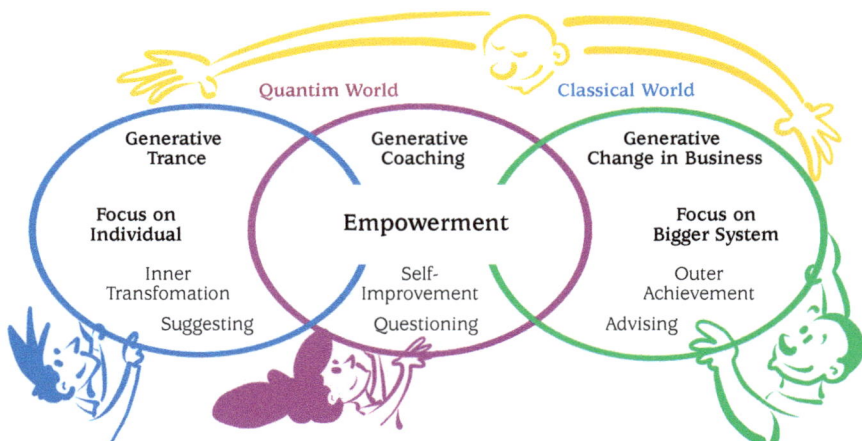

The Intersection Between Generative Trance, Generative Coaching and Generative Change in Business

The Six-Step Model of Generative Coaching

For the remainder of this book, we will focus on the process and competences of Generative Coaching.

One of our basic definitions of generative coaching is: *The art of using the "disciplined flow" of creative consciousness to generate new identities and realities.* This definition implies that, while it is grounded in concrete behavioral expressions, Generative Coaching is directed toward deep and fundamental levels of creative change. The term "disciplined flow" captures the notion of complementarity between the concrete, classical world and the quantum field that is at the heart of Generative Change and Generative Coaching.

As we have pointed out in the previous chapter, the Generative Change work that we have been developing over the last 20 years can be expressed in a core prototype that we call the Six-Step Model. This model is something that took us quite a few years to really perfect. And the power of it is that it is, on one hand, a very clear step-by-step process. On the other hand, it is not rigid. It actually allows for a lot of both flexibility and the inclusion of many different methods and modalities to satisfy any particular step. It is a good example of what we mean by "disciplined flow."

In all generative change work, the organizing principle is creativity. In our view, the creative process has six different fundamental parts to it. By looking at these parts individually and then in relationship to each other, you can fluidly, but in a very disciplined way, achieve amazing and creative results.

The Six-Steps of Generative Coaching parallel the deep structure prototype of all generative change:

1. Open a COACH field
2. Set a positive intention/direction
3. Develop a generative (creative) state
4. Take action
5. Transform obstacles/resistances
6. Establish practices for continued creativity

In **step one**, you're grounding in yourself and opening to the quantum field.

Open a COACH field

In **step two**, you're picking a direction within that field of all possibilities. You are deciding, "What is it that I want to manifest in my life now."

Set a positive intention/direction

Step three involves connecting out to the parts of your field of resources that you are going to need to help you move creatively and effectively towards your desired state.

Develop a generative (creative) state

Step four is about moving into action. And that's almost invariably where you will start to face the obstacles and interferences.

Take action

Transform obstacles/resistances

So, **step five** is about meeting and interacting with those obstacles while staying connected to the generative state and the COACH field in order to transform them. What typically happens when we meet an obstacle is that some part of our generative state starts to collapses. Our attention retracts. We lose a sense of our direction. We lose the connection to ourselves. So, step five is crucial for success in the coaching process.

Step six is about establishing practices for deepening the changes you have started in the coaching session. How many of your mothers told you, "Sweetheart, you're only as good as your practices?" Probably not many of them. So, let us be your honorary mothers and say, "You're only as good as your practices." When you're doing generative change sessions, whether it's with an individual or group, nothing has changed yet from this session. What the session has awakened is a possibility. But it's not actual yet. So, for you to be able to translate that possibility into a reality, you need to have commitment and practices.

Establish practices for continued creativity

In the coming chapters of this book, we will go over each of these steps of the Generative Coaching process in depth. We will provide you with more information and examples of how to accomplish each step in a variety of ways. As you will learn, each step is a journey in and of itself. And, while they provide a clear path, it is not necessary to follow these steps in a rigid way.

We look forward to sharing our more than 80 years of combined experience with you.

There is a vitality, a life force, a quickening that is translated through you into action, and because there is only one of you in all time, this expression is unique.

If you block it, it will never exist through any other medium and be lost.

The world will not have it.

It is not yours to determine how good it is; nor how it compares with other expressions.

It is your business to keep the channel open.

– Martha Graham

Chapter 3

Step 1
Opening the COACH field

The first, and perhaps most important, step in the generative coaching process is to "open a COACH field." What this means is for both the coach and client to be in a shared state of resonance where creative ideas can easily emerge as a result of the interaction between them. In this state and relationship, both coach and client have access to insights beyond conscious, cognitive limitations.

To reach it, you have to relax, you have to ground, and you have to open up. You've got to make this connection that, *"I'm not an isolated box but I'm part of a larger creative field of amazing consciousness."*

In the quote at the beginning of this chapter, the famous dancer Martha Graham talks about the importance of "keeping your channel open." The first step in generative coaching is about opening that channel – being Centered, Open, Aware, Connected and able to Hold whatever is happening from a place of hospitality, resourcefulness, curiosity, and creativity.

Practicing The COACH State: Opening the Channel

The following is a basic prototype that can be used to guide yourself or someone else into a COACH state.

1. Sit or stand in a comfortable position with both feet flat on the floor and your spine erect but relaxed (i.e., "in your vertical axis"). Check that your breathing is regular and from the belly. (Short, rapid breathing from the chest would indicate that you are in a stressed mode.)

2. Bring your attention to the soles of your feet (i.e., put your "mind" into your feet.). Become aware of the universe of sensations in the bottoms of your feet. Feel the surface of your heels, toes, arches and the balls of your feet.

3. Begin to expand your awareness to include the physical volume (the 3-dimensional space) of your feet and then move your awareness up through your lower legs, knees, thighs, pelvis and hips. Become aware of your belly center, breathe deeply into it and say to yourself: *"I am here." "I am present." "I am centered."*

4. Continuing to stay aware of your lower body, expand your awareness up through your solar plexus, spine, lungs, rib cage and chest. Bring awareness to your heart center in your upper chest, breathe into your chest and say to yourself: *"I am open." "I am opening."*

5. Now continue to expand your awareness up through your shoulders, upper arms, elbows, lower arms, wrists, hands and fingers, and up through your neck, throat and face. Be sure to include all of the senses in the head: the eyes, ears, nose, mouth and tongue. Bring your awareness to the skull, brain and the center in your head, behind your eyes. Breathe as if you are breathing into your head center, brining oxygen and energy, and say to yourself: *"I am awake." "I am aware." "I am alert and clear."*

6. Staying in contact with the ongoing physical sensations in your body, starting from your feet and including all three centers (belly, heart and head), become aware of all of the space below you, going into the center of the Earth, all the space above you, reaching into the sky; all of the space to your left; all of the space to your right; all of the space behind you; all of the space in front of

you. Feel a deep sense of connection to your feet and the centers in your belly, heart and head, and to the environment and field around you. Be aware of the vast array of resources available to you within yourself and in the field around you. When you can experience a connection to this sense of a larger Self, say to yourself, *"I am connected."*

7. Keeping your awareness on your body and simultaneously on the space around you, sense a type of field or holding environment in which you can hold all of the resources, strength, intelligence and wisdom available to you as well as disturbing energies such as fear, anger, sadness, etc. Feel the sense of courage and confidence to face whatever comes your way as you stay centered and present with all of yourself and open to your environment. Say to yourself, *"I am ready." "I can hold whatever is here with curiosity, resourcefulness and creativity."*

Both the coach and client enter a shared state of resonance where creative ideas can easily emerge as a result the interaction between them.

Introducing the COACH State in a Coaching Context

There are many ways to introduce the COACH state to a client in the coaching context. In actuality, the way that a Generative Coaching conversation might typically begin is a person comes in and there might be a little informal conversation and some discussion about what they would like to do in the session. Then, as a generative coach, we would say, *"Great, I really want to support you in that. And I think a good first step is to make sure that you get into your best possible state so that you can make creative movement towards that goal."* The generative coach might explain, *"The reason I'm asking you to do this is because there's something that you want, and you need a positive connection with yourself and your inner resources in order to get there. So in order to do that, I'd like to suggest that we start by making those positive connections."*

We have never had a client say, *"I don't think that's a good idea."*

We have had a lot of clients who say, *"Great, but how?"*

The good news is that everyone actually already at some level knows how. We would say that what we are calling the COACH state is a psycho-biologically necessary state. We have a psycho-biological need to let go of our isolated ego and go into this larger experience of connection with the world. So in Generative Coaching we don't narrowly focus on the COACH state as an artificial technique. What we're really interested in is how does the client do that already in his or her own life?

For example, as a coach, you can ask, *"When you need to relax, what do you do? What do you need to tune in to?"* *"When you need to reconnect with yourself after you've been working 40 days and 40 nights, what are some of the things you do?"* We search for those places and then we help clients to experience these situations very actively.

We will get answers such as: I do yoga, listen to music, play with my kids, ride my horse or my bicycle, dance, walk in the woods, sing, practice Aikido, swim, read, meditate, etc. These are typical ways that people reconnect with themselves and their inner resources, and are a good lead in to how to enter a COACH state.

Revivifying the Client's COACH Experiences

Once a client has identified such an example, we help them to deepen their experience of it by asking questions such as, *"What are you aware of going on inside of you when you experience that? How and where in your body do you feel your connection with yourself and your inner resources? What are some of the qualities that characterize your inner state of being in that experience?"*

We call this process **"Revivifying the client's COACH experiences."** The basic prototype of the method is:

1. Settle in, settle down.

2. Set an intention to open a COACH field.

3. Ask the client to identify COACH experiences in his or her personal life (e.g., experiences of resourcefulness, resilience, flow, connection, etc.) or develop an imaginary scenario.

4. Ask client to slowly describe specific internal sensory elements of the experience, pausing periodically to breathe them through his or her body.

5. Feed back the client's description, experiencing them yourself in order to unfold a parallel state in you.

Demonstration of Revivifying the Client's COACH Experiences

The following transcript from a coaching session Steve did in one of our programs provides a good illustration of how this can be done.

Steve: *So let's just see what might be the best way to work together so that you would walk away from here with the sense of, "That really was interesting and useful."*

Client: *Okay.*

Steve: *Do you have an idea right at the outset in terms of what goal or intention would be really good to begin to set our conversation around?*

Client: *Yeah. To be graceful and grateful.*

Steve: *To be grateful in any particular area of your life? Where would grace and gratitude be really helpful for you and maybe other people?*

Client: *I think it's both at work and at home. I think, for me, it is about being grateful for who we are. So helping others and myself to be grateful for who we are and for all that we are.*

Steve: *And I am just curious, if there was one color image in which you were seeing yourself in your life or were seeing the world from this place of greater gratitude, what would it be? Is there any particular image coming to mind?*

Client: *The image that comes to mind straight away is of an Alpine meadow, with lovely daisies, and flowers, and grasses, and a blue sky.*

Steve: *Awesome. To help activate the best place to experience the gratitude and anything else that might go with that, is there anything else that could help you to find the best connection with yourself?*

Client: *Standing up and feeling the earth beneath my feet.*

Steve: *Let's do that.* (Both stand up.) *And maybe you can connect here for a few moments* (points to belly center).

Client: *Yeah.* (Takes a deep breath.)

Steve: *I am just wondering, it seemed like you opened a little bit of space within you and I was hoping that we could use it to get a little connection between us as well. That way, I could support whatever it is that you want to do. What does that touch in you?*

Client: *A calmness. A very.~ yeah, just a very gentle and calm place ~ yeah.*

Steve: *So I'd like to say to that place sincerely, "Hi".*

Client: (Smiles broadly.) *Hi.*

Revivifying the client's COACH state experience

1) ASK: WHAT DO YOU WANT?

2) Fully reconnect to a memory of naturally being in a COACH state.

3) Develop a relational resonance Field between Coach and Client to activate a COACH Field

Deepening the COACH State

Starting with these resourceful experiences is a good beginning. It is also important for us to point out here that almost inevitably people's first understanding of the COACH state is that it should always be a positive feeling or a state of complete serenity. But we want to clarify early on that is not just a positive feeling state. That would be too shallow. Because in any meaningful challenge you face, you'll have to deal with much more than the positive stuff. So, in a true COACH state, you will have what the Buddhists call "equanimity," which means having the same quality of presence and resourcefulness whether there is joy or there's suffering. And to deal with any really difficult challenge, you need that ability.

Remember, the COACH state is not related to any particular emotional response. It is a function of the state of our somatic, cognitive and relational filters. The state of these filters determines how we experience, process and express whatever is coming through them.

The point is that, in a COACH state, I certainly could feel joy. I can also be in a COACH state and feel sadness. And I can be in a COACH state and feel frustration. And I can be in a COACH state and experience anger. The question is what happens to that anger, frustration, joy or sadness? When I hold them in the COACH state, the form through which they express has many possibilities. If I took the same feelings – frustration, anger, joy or sadness – and held them in a CRASH state, nothing very generative would come through. But if I take the same frustration, and I center, open, bring awareness and stay connected to my resources, something really creative and useful can emerge.

One of our core principles of Generative Coaching is that *"no content has a fixed expression or meaning in and of itself."* Whether it's an emotion, or a thought, or a feeling, it is not inherently positive or negative. What makes a particular response a problem or a resource is your relationship with it and the state of your filters as you interact with it.

This goes back to the notion of the big circle and the little circle that we presented in Chapter 1. In a generative conversation, the COACH state is the big circle and whatever content is brought up by conversation – the present state, the desired state, the obstacles, the resources, etc. – is the content of the little circle

So in Generative Coaching we're helping clients realize that the states of well-being that they know how to access under the best conditions also need to be available and accessible to them under the most adversarial circumstances. And this is one of the things they can really learn how to do through the Generative Coaching process.

For example, if you take fear and you hold it in a COACH state, you often get something like heightened awareness. The fear is there, but you're connected to something bigger than the fear. In a CRASH state if you have fear, you end up in panic. It is the same fear but the way that your filters hold it will determine how the energy becomes expressed.

This is why we say that, anything that's going to come up in a Generative Coaching session, we always want to meet it first in a COACH state.

In a generative conversation, the COACH state is the big circle and whatever content is brought up by conversation is the content of the little circle

It is not uncommon for a client to say, *"Here's what I want,"* and then start to get anxious, or start to doubt. One of the most common occurrences is what we call "Yes, but. . ." The client says, *"This is what I want,"* but somebody else inside says, *"Well I don't."* Part of what we are talking about as a COACH field is creating a conversational space that can welcome and hold all of these possible responses.

One way to talk about what you're doing at this first step is "gathering the team." As we pointed out in our previous chapters, generativity requires multiple complementary parts (some of which initially seem contradictory). We need dreamer, realist and critic. We need representatives from all parts of the "holon" – young parts, mature parts, confident parts, fearful parts, etc. We need to make space for all of them.

So in this first step of creating a COACH field, you're getting all of the team there. Given what the client wants to create, we're trying to welcome all of the players and "get them together at the tea ceremony," so that everybody is respected, and nobody's monopolizing the microphone. If you only get part of the team, you will run into problems later on. As part of this first phase we're always trying to welcome whatever's there, because whatever is not welcomed in this first step is going to show up later as a resistance, an interference or an obstacle. Whatever you leave out is going to eventually go *"Wait a minute. What about me?"*

Self-Calibration and Self-Scaling

Some of those team members may show up in a CRASH form at first. *"I'm anxious about this,"* or *"I don't know, I tried this before and it went badly."* That is why one thing we like to do, especially in this first step, is to help the client learn **"self-calibration."** This means being aware of how much I am in or am not in a particular mindset, or a particular state. We like to use the process of "self-scaling" as a way to help a person begin to calibrate the level of their COACH state. So we'll take the COACH state or the various elements of the COACH state, and put them on a scale of 0 to 10. On this scale, "0" is *"I am completely in a CRASH state"* and "10" is *"I'm in the most grounded and open COACH state I've ever been in."* We then help the client to sense, *"Where am I on that scale?"* at various points in the coaching session.

One of our core principles is that it's impossible and probably not even desirable to be at the level of 10 all of the time. In fact, we would say **"the optimum is not always the maximum."** You don't always want to drive your car at full speed. So what we are looking for is a zone, we call it a *"zone of excellence"* or zone of generativity. Rather than a fixed point, this zone identifies a range within the scale where you are still able to be resourceful and potentially generative. Typically this range with respect to the COACH state is at least 7 out of 10 or above. If it starts dropping below 5, 4 or 3, the person is going into CRASH, and essentially, the channel is closing. The filters are closing down.

You will produce negative experiences and behaviors if you're trying to do something challenging from a low level of COACH state. If you ask your client, *"How much of a positive connection do you feel to yourself right now?"* and the person says *"Three,"* then to continue is not going to produce anything positive or generative. They have to first upgrade their state so that they're in a place where they can trust themselves and stay open to the world around them.

So we put the COACH state on a sliding scale. It's not all or nothing. In fact, the level of a client's COACH state can really vary quite a bit during a session. So being able to track what is happening through the self-scaling process is really helpful in the session. It tells the coach, "Are we ready for the next step?" Or "Do we need to bring resources in?"

In many ways, self-scaling is even more helpful as a tool that clients can use in their everyday experience. It's a great thing to learn to know how much access I have to my COACH state at any point in time. If I know where I am in my inner state, I have a possibility of being able to adjust it. So I'm able to put myself in the best conditions for success.

Here is the prototypic process we use for learning to use self-scaling with the COACH state.

Optimizing the COACH State

1. Using a 0-10 scale, let a number come that represents the present level of your COACH state (where 0 would indicate a complete CRASH state and 10 would represent being fully in a state of flow).

2. Explore what you can do to increase your COACH state just a little bit more (i.e., physical, verbal, visual, reference experience, role model, acting "as if," etc.)

3. What level does it move to?

4. What difference does it make? What becomes possible now?

5. How could you "anchor" this level of resourcefulness so that it is available to you in the future?

It is important to learn to know how much access you have to your COACH state at any point in time.

Demonstration of Optimizing the COACH State

The following transcript, from a coaching session Robert did in one of our programs, provides a good illustration of how this can be done.

Robert: *So, I am curious, as we start the process, what is your intention for this session.*

Client: *For me it is very important to create a strong and consistent state to develop my project.*

Robert: *Great. That's interesting because that is exactly what we are going to do in this first step. We are going to explore how you could really work to create a strong and consistent COACH state. In fact, part of what we are going to be doing is to explore how to recognize the level of that COACH state and strengthen the parts that need to be strengthened. So that makes me curious about whether you have a reference experience for being in a resourceful and creative state.*

Client: *When I did my own training program about leadership, I had this strong feeling of this state. There were 7,000 people there and I brought 100 trainers to the program. It was an Evening Youth Program. And it was really like the strongest COACH field and a lot of young people with burning and clever eyes.*

Robert: *I just want to say to you that as you share that, I feel that a shiver and a light that goes through me. So, let's take a moment and, as you really pause and put yourself back into that experience and breathe that through you, where do you sense it most in your body?*

Client: *It's like an energy that comes through my body from down below my feet, from the Earth and through my body, and goes somewhere.*

Robert: *And I see that a smile comes out on your face. Does the energy have any color or any temperature?*

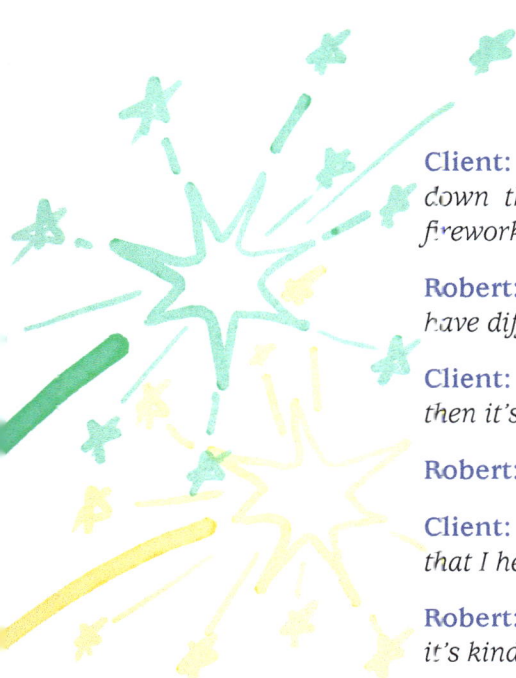

Client: *Yes. When this energy comes from down there, it is white and then it's like fireworks in all directions.*

Robert: *And you said it's white. Does it also have different colors?*

Client: *Yes. It comes up to here as white and then it's all colored.*

Robert: *Are you aware of anything else?*

Client: *It's like music, some kind of music that I hear.*

Robert: *Music? That's interesting. You say it's kind of like music. What do you hear?*

Client: *It resembles good rock music.*

Robert: *OK, now I get it. Fantastic. Let's take a moment and really be with that. One of the things I want to do is that if we start to make a scale of 0 to 10, where zero is "I am not in my generative COACH state at all" and 10 is "I am in the best one I've ever been." When you check inside right now, and if you let the number come as to what level you're in right now. What would it be?*

Client: *It's 8.5.*

Robert: *Great. Lovely to see 8.5. First of all, one question. Where did that number come from? How did you know that? Because it's interesting, they come from different places in us.*

Client: *From down side up. But the center is here.* (Points to heart.)

Robert: *Just out of curiosity, 8.5 is already pretty high, but if you were going to make it just even a little bit more, what do you need to do?*

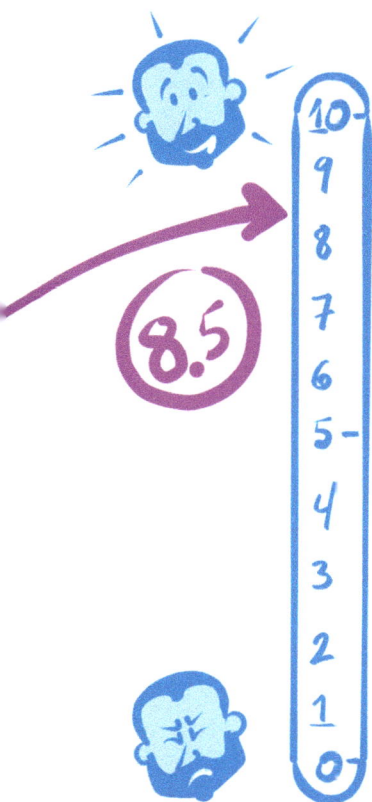

Client: (Begins to stretch and lengthen his spine.)

Robert: *Ah, that's interesting. Something with your body. I point that out because you said that part of your intention is you want to be able to have a consistent strong COACH state. So what did you just do? What were you aware of?*

Client: *I want to stand up in some sense.*

Robert: *Shall we?*

Client: (Stands up. Robert follows.) *That's better.*

Robert: *What's shifted for you?*

Client: *It's much easier to come even deeper in that state. It's like 9.*

Robert: *And how do you know? What makes it easier?*

Client: *There is this feeling that this energy passes through. And there are a lot of beautiful people with clever eyes out there* (points to audience). *And it really resembles that experience.*

Robert: *Fantastic. So, just to comment. Why am I asking for all of these details? Because in this moment it's nice. We are able to get a good resourceful state in this moment. But what's going to happen through the course of the session is we are going to meet obstacles and we are going to need all of these reminders. These gestures. This image. This music. These all become anchors that you can use to get that state back in challenging situations.*

And, in fact, for a practice, when you said you set that as your intention, were you thinking of certain other situations where it is not so natural and easy for you to have this resourceful state?

Client: When I get tired. I have a lot of trainings and consulting sessions. And besides I have to develop my own project. Then I give a lot of energy away.

Robert: As you say that, it is easy to see that the CRASH is coming. So, right now, as you think about those situations, what level does your COACH state go to?

Client: Something like 4.

Robert: One thing that we usually say in the generative coaching process is that, of course, it's great if your COACH state is up to 8.5 and 9. But you don't have to be perfect in order to still be generative. We would usually say if it starts to get below 7 out of 10, your creative ability starts to drop off rapidly. So, in these training situations where you've been working a lot, it would be kind of hard to demand "I should always be at 10!" But 4 is probably going start to make things worse. So, the thing I'd be interested in exploring with you is what you could do bring the level of your COACH state back up. When you tune into being centered, open, aware and connected, which of those seems the weakest when you are at 4? Is it more that "I've lost my center" or "I am not as open or as aware?" It could be, of course, a combination.

I ask this, because part of what we are always trying to do in Generative Coaching is increase our own self-awareness. If I am not aware of something, there is nothing I can do about it. I have no choice about it. But, even in that CRASH state, if I can be aware of what's happening, I can start to actually have a choice. Do I want to stay here or would I want to be a little bit more centered or more open? So, what would you say in those situations? What would it be?

Client: *I start to disconnect from the outside world, I am in some kind of cocoon.*

Robert: *So, first of all, I want to say to the cocoon "Welcome." I am sure it makes sense. I am putting out so much out there, some part of me just wants to disconnect. So, welcome. I am sure it's there for a really good reason. It is wanting to do something very positive. If you welcomed the cocoon, what would you become aware of?*

Client: *It helps me to relax and rejuvenate*

Robert: *To relax. That's interesting. To rejuvenate. So, that's interesting. What it is really doing is not trying to make you more disconnected and more tired.*

Client: *No. It is telling me that it is time to recharge.*

Robert: *It is telling you that it is time to recharge. That's good. That's interesting. Good to know. And I am curious if instead of having your COACH state go down all the way to 4, if you could hold that intention to recharge and stay centered, stay opened, and stay connected, what do you connect to that helps you to recharge?*

Client: *I think it is with my dream, my idea, with the world and with the people.*

Robert: *So we have two very powerful and interesting images here. One is the fireworks and the other is the cocoon. What happens to the fireworks when you go to the cocoon?*

Client: *It kind of stops and stays around here.* (Gestures to his solar plexus.)

Robert: *That's interesting. And how does it know that it's time to come back?*

Client: *The cocoon kind of melts. And then the fireworks starts again.*

Robert: *That's interesting. I am curious, if you were to make your somatic model of the cocoon, what would that be?* (Client folds arms and bends forward.)

That's interesting. And what's your somatic model for the fireworks? (Client reaches his arms over his head and leans back.)

That's interesting. And right now, these two things are disconnected.

And we notice something very interesting. If my intention is to be this (reaches arms over his head and leans back) *all the time, what happens? This* (folds arms and bends forward) *comes in. One is the complement of the other. I am wondering if instead of doing so much of this* (reaches arms over his head and leans back), *that you have to do this* (folds arms and bends forward) – *what if you kind of smoothly go back and forth between those two? What would that be like?*

Client: (Begins to move back and forth between the two gestures.) *It resembles swimming.*

Robert: (Mirrors the movement.) *It's swimming.*

Client: *When we make a movement and then allow ourselves to glide on the water and have some rest.*

Robert: *That's interesting.*

Client: *That's great.*

Robert: *Now, when you think about doing all of those sessions you were talking about earlier, if you could swim through those sessions, what would that be like?*

Client: *I have a thought that sometimes I do it in this way. But sometimes I want to swim even faster and I make a lot of unnecessary movements and effort.*

Robert: *That's interesting. Let's welcome that too. There is something in you that wants to swim faster and makes unnecessary movements. Welcome. Where does that part of you that wants to go faster live inside of you?*

Client: *I feel like a direction vector, from the solar plexus and that kind of movement.* (Makes a rapid gesture with right hand and arm out from the solar plexus.)

Robert: *Welcome.*

Client: *And it has a word "Forwards."*

Robert: *Welcome to another team member. I am curious, if you could make that gesture a little more slowly and from a COACH state, honoring this intention to go forward, what would happen.*

Client: (Makes the gesture more slowly, pausing between each movement.) *It's like a boat when you row, or after the movement, it kind of glides on the water. And it's an easy and resourceful and free movement.*

Robert: *I know from rowing myself that if you move the paddles too fast you do not actually go faster. You need to give it that time to glide. So, I'm curious right now, if you turn into these fireworks, to the cocoon, this desire to go forward, and you make that rowing motion, what happens?*

Client: (Makes a smooth and rhythmic rowing movement.) *There is a boat that easily glides on the water and there's lot of fireworks all around the boat. And it is also like a walk that brings you pleasure and joy.*

Robert: *So, let's check again about thinking of these times when you are doing a lot of sessions. A few minutes ago when you were thinking them, your COACH state went down to 4. What happens now when you think about those same situations?*

Client: *I want to make a small rowing motion and enjoy the movement of the boat and then to do this (makes rowing gesture) again and easily glide on the water. And it is really resourceful.*

Robert: *What number would you say your COACH state is at when you do that?*

Client: *9.5. We'll leave this half a point for the future. (Smiles broadly.)*

Optimizing the COACH state

3) LET THE
BODY GUIDE
YOU. WHAT
HAPPENS WHEN
YOU GO SLOWLY
FROM ONE
STATE TO THE
OTHER?

1) HELP THE
CLIENT TO
ACCESS THEIR
COACH STATE
AT AN OPTIMUM
LEVEL

2)
CONTRAST
WITH A
SITUATION
WHERE THE
COACH
STATE IS
BELOW 7.

TO DO

6) **Integrate into a new optimized state.**

4) **Explore the positive intention of the less resourceful state.**

9.5

5) **Welcome any other part that has a message.**

FORWARDS

This demonstration illustrates how often, in the beginning, people will have a fixed map of what the COACH state is. In this case it was something like fireworks. But if we think about what happens to fireworks: they burn out. So they were balanced by the "cocoon", whose intention was to rejuvenate. A generative process always involves this type of conversation between opposites. Referencing Chinese philosophy, we can say that your Yang needs to be balanced by your Yin. A big part of what we want to do in Generative Coaching is put these representations back into a more flexible state. So instead of fireworks versus a cocoon, we have something like swimming. It is a new and a different representation. Bringing them together in a COACH state allows us to include both parts in a new representation.

In this case, there was another part that wanted to go forward quickly. But trying to go forward too quickly was also going to trigger to the cocoon reaction. And again, rather than try to get rid of it, we say *"Welcome. What's your representation of that? How can we adjust your COACH filters to include that part and put its expression into a more fluid state?"*

We will be exploring this dynamic between complementarities further in our chapter on step 5, which is about transforming obstacles.

Strengthening the COACH Field

In both of the demonstrations presented in this chapter Steve and Robert mirror the gestures and movements of their clients and feed back things that the clients have said. That has to do with this notion of creating a COACH field, which emerges from the resonance between the states of the coach and client. If the coach is just sitting and watching the client make his or her gesture, then it's "me and him/her." "Me" and "you" are separate. **What we want to create is the field of "we".** This is also why we will often share with our clients some of the things that are happening inside of us as a coach when the client is speaking or making his or her gesture. A COACH field is always a "we", it's not "your state" and "my state," it's "our state."

Once a client has begun to get an understanding and some good reference experiences for the COACH state, a stronger COACH field between coach and client can be developed through practices like the following.

Strengthening the COACH Field

1. Sit facing each other in a relaxed, aligned and balanced posture

2. Bring your awareness into your body and your breath and become present.

3. Keeping eye contact, take turns making the following declarations to each other:

   I invite the quality of centeredness into myself and into the space of the relationship between us.

   I invite the energy of openness into myself and into the space of the relationship between us.

   I invite greater awareness into myself and into the space of the relationship between us.

   I invite a greater sense of connection with myself and into the relationship between us.

   I am committed to holding whatever emerges within myself and within the space of our relationship.

4. Share with each other what you sense is present in the field of your relationship; e.g., *"I sense both strength and sadness in the space between us."*

5. Set your intention for the duration of the interaction you will be having; e.g., *"My intention is to stay in connection with my creativity and my humor throughout our interaction today."*

Once a robust COACH field has been created by the coach and client (a level of 7 or more out of 10), you are ready to go on to step 2: Clarifying and setting the intention for the coaching session.

It is important to keep in mind, however, that we do not forget about the COACH state and the COACH field after step 1. On the contrary, it is always the primary focus of a good generative coach. We like to point out that, if the client's COACH state has dropped below 7, you have about five seconds to help them return to COACH state before they go over a tipping point and their capacity for resilience disappears. If the client starts spiraling down to 5, 4, 3, etc., and gets into strong CRASH state, you essentially have to stop and reset the whole interaction.

Look beyond yourself.
The keys to your heart's desire
lie beyond the eyes and ears you hold
against the world
and cannot be claimed even
in the rightings of all the wrongs
you have suffered in your life.

The past
is not a path to fulfillment.
Your history is for lessons
and not for life.

Passion lives
in the present
and
in the future
now waiting for you
ready to deliver
your deepest wish.

~ Nick LeForce

Chapter 4

Step 2
Setting Intentions/Goals

Step two of our six steps of generative coaching is about setting an intention. The purpose of setting an intention is to activate our creative consciousness towards a positive, meaningful future by defining a clear direction. Even if you don't yet know the details of your destination, you want to set your direction. The question we typically ask is, "What do you most want to create in your life?" This is a crucial step of the Generative Coaching process. What is the positive, meaningful future you want to bring into the world? As Nick LeForce says in the poem above, "Passion lives in the present and in the future now waiting to deliver your deepest wish." In Generative Coaching we want to work with that deepest wish.

The word "intention" is derived from the Latin *intendere*, which literally means "to stretch out" or "extend." *Intention* is typically defined as "the purpose, end or aim toward which thoughts are directed"; or "an anticipated outcome that guides your planned actions." It is also used to mean "a determination to act in a certain way." Thus, intentions are what we want or hope to accomplish through our activity.

A person with the intention "to help," for instance, may not know exactly what he or she is going to do or will need to do, but is ready and willing to engage in any number of specific actions which may satisfy that general intention. In this way, intentions are generative.

Nobel prize laureate Mohammad Yunus is a good example of this. When his native country of Bangladesh became an independent nation in the early 1970's Yunus returned from studying in the United States with the intention to help the many impoverished people in his country. He did not know what he would do. He only knew that he intended to find a way to help. In 1976, during visits to the poorest households in a local village, Yunus discovered that very small loans could make a disproportionate difference to a poor person. Yunus lent US$27 of his money to 42 women in the village to buy bamboo to make bamboo furniture. Working together and supporting each other, they were able to pay the loan back and still make a good profit. Yunus eventually developed this approach into the concept of microcredit for which he received the 2006 Nobel Peace Prize. His intention "to help" guided him to create a whole new model for social business.

Similarly, the intention to "bring positive energy" or to "stay centered" can have many different specific expressions. From this perspective, an intention is a type of filter that directs our attention and brings certain resources, skills and actions into the foreground.

Defining an Intention for Generative Change

As we have pointed out, the purpose of step 2 to is to help the client orient their focus toward creating a positive and meaningful future for themselves and others. The types of questions we usually ask are things like:

* What do you most want to create?

* What is your vision or dream for a better life?

* What are you being called to do or become?

* What is your deepest longing?

To make an intention actionable in a coaching session it needs to be directed towards some context or application domain. In our Generative Coaching work, we identify three basic application domains for creative intention.

1. **Professional life** – work relationships, relationship to money, time, etc.

2. **Personal relationships** – family, intimacy relationships, children, friends, etc.

3. **Relationship with self** – body, health, future self, past self, etc.

An intention can be directed to relationship with self, personal relationships or profesional life

Lessons from the Dying

Sometimes, to help a client get a sense of a meaningful intention, we will ask about the opposite: "What would you regret not doing or creating in your life?" Bronnie Ware is an Australian nurse who spent several years working in palliative care, caring for patients in the last 12 weeks of their lives. In her book *The Top Five Regrets of the Dying*, she recorded her conversations with people about any regrets they had or what they would do differently in their lives. Most had not honored even half of their dreams. They went to their death realizing that this was a choice they had made, and they deeply regretted having never really lived their dreams, or even part of them. As Irish playwright George Bernard Shaw said, *"most people go to their graves with their music still in them."* The top five regrets were:

1. I wish I'd had the courage to *live a life true to myself*, not the one others expected of me.

2. I wish that *I hadn't worked so hard*.

3. I wish I'd had the courage to *express my feelings.*

4. I wish I had *stayed in touch with my friends*.

5. I wish I had *let myself be happier*.

Reflecting on these areas of regret can often give guidance for clients to examine areas of their lives where they are not currently being generative.

Not to tight. Not too loose.

An essential aspect of doing step 2 effectively is how to represent and express the intention once it has been established. There is a wise saying that *"energy flows where attention goes."* Where we put our attention determines what we give our energy to. If an intention is defined too narrowly, there is no room for creative energy. If an intention is too vague and ungrounded, there is nowhere for creative energy to be directed.

Errol Flynn, the star of a number of classic Hollywood swashbuckling films in the Golden Age of Movies, was actually quite an accomplished swordsman. When asked how to hold a sword correctly the actor replied "in the same way you would hold a bird, not too tight and not too loose. If you hold it too tightly the bird dies, but if you hold too loosely it will fly away and you're left with nothing."

This is a good metaphor for how to hold an intention for Generative Change. If it is too specific and detailed, there is no room for generativity. If it is too ungrounded and vague, there is no direction for creative action. We like to say that the intention should be "shimmering." That means that it has a definite shape but not a rigid and fixed form. We are always looking for that balance that gives us the possibility for "disciplined flow."

Traditional coaching applies well-formedness conditions to goal setting such as being SMART: Specific, Measurable, Achievable, Relevant, and Time-Bound. An example might be, *"I want to lose two kilograms in the next two weeks."* This, of course, is fine for traditional coaching but it is like saying, *"I want to get my first cup of coffee or tea by 9am tomorrow morning."* There is not much generativity involved or required. There are many goals that do not require creativity.

By contrast, in the example cited earlier, Mohammad Yunus would not have been able to say, "I want to go to Bangladesh and invent microcredit in 1976 and get a Nobel prize by 2006."

In Generative Coaching we are always looking for that balance of the intention being specific enough to engage creative action, yet open enough to include many possibilities.

So, if a client is too specific about their intention, we will ask, *"What will that do for you?"* For example, if a client says, *"I want to lose two kilograms in the next two weeks,"* we would ask, *"What will it do for you to lose two kilograms in the next two weeks?"* The client might answer something like, *"I would have more energy and feel more of a sense of inner balance."* This can then become an intention that has many other possible expressions and manifestations.

If a client is too vague about their intention, we will ask, *"What would be a concrete situation and example of that intention?"* For instance, if a client says their intention is *"connection,"* we would ask, *"Who or what is most important for you to connect to?"* Perhaps the client would answer, *"I want to reconnect with my daughter."* This can then become a source for creative actions.

Representing an Intention for Generative Change

In a Generative Coaching session, you will typically sit down with the client and talk informally a little bit about what they want to achieve in the session. Most people need to talk a little bit just informally. Then we would start shifting more formally to step 1 and create a good COACH field. From there, we go into what might be called the *formal representation of their intention* for the Generative Coaching session. This "formal" representation of an intention for Generative Change has three key conditions. It needs to include the following three modalities:

1. Verbal statement
(positive, succinct, resonant)

2. Visual image
(color, literal or symbolic)

3. Somatic model
(posture, gesture and movement)

To initiate creative action, you have to verbalize the intention, you have to envision it and you have to embody it in order to sustain it. Because you're going to get a lot of resistance to any type of significant change. So, if you are holding the intention in only one modality – words, visual images or somatic expressions – chances are you will lose it very early on the path.

In traditional coaching people often just represent their desired state with words. There's this idea if you get more detail in words than your outcome is somehow clearer. We generally find, however, that when we start getting more words, the intention becomes either less clear or more disconnected from emotions and actions. So, this is where we want to engage multiple intelligences.

Thus, once a good COACH state has been established, the generative coach would say, *"Now, let's tune into this intention a little bit more. I'm going to ask you to express it with simple positive words."* Now positive doesn't simply mean good. It means, *"What is it that you actually want to create, achieve or experience?"*

If somebody says, *"Well, I want to stop doing this"* or *"I want to not do something"* we ask, *"So, what do you want?"* That's what we mean by positive. **It's towards something meaningful that the client wants,** as opposed to simply away from something they do not want. If a client said, *"I just want to not feel so bad in my intimate relationship,"* we would ask, *"So what type of satisfying relationship with your intimate partner do you really want to create?"*

Another implication of the notion of "positive" is that it is something deeply and personally meaningful to the client, and not simply a superficial action or achievement. If a client's intention is "to change others" or "to achieve success" or "just get rid of pain," we ask *"What difference would that make in your sense of self? What would that give you that's important?"* For example, the client might realize *"If I wasn't so anxious, I would feel more calm and trusting." "If I could make my daughter stop using drugs, I would feel self-love as a mother."* This helps to direct the client's attention and creative energy towards a more complete "holon" of their existence.

The second condition is that **the verbal statement needs to be succinct.** And we have a little rule in Generative Coaching: you've got five words maximum for the formal statement of the intention. We prompt the client to say, *"What I really want to create is . . ."* and from that point on they've got five words. We give the client the first part of the statement for free. Those prompt words don't count as part of the five-word limit. But once they get to the end of the diving board – "What I really want to create is . . ." – we usually will just hold a hand up and count with our fingers how many words are used. This is because the majority of people quickly exceed the limit. We'll humorously say, *"Beep. I'm sorry. You've exceeded the limit. Try again."*

The reason that we do this is that it's really important to focus attention on the intention and say it as simply as possible. When you start using a lot of words, what's happening is you're essentially moving up into just the cognitive mind. You start diluting the intention with *"I'd like to but . . . and then it may be this too."* Or *"Let me explain a little bit more about this part and . . ."* So, all of that is diluting the power of the intention.

Not only that, but all the research shows that you forget after you get past about 9 words. So, if I tell you what I want in 150 words and tomorrow you ask, *"What was that you wanted again?"* People will answer, *"Well, the thing I wanted was … what was that? I don't know, something about happiness."* One word. So, we want to focus on those few key words that people will remember over an extended period of time.

This is why we have the third condition that **the words have to be resonant in the body**. This is one of the most important research findings, that the words have magical power when they resonate somewhere in the body. So, we want the statement of the intention to be positive, succinct and resonant. As a client is verbalizing their intention, you have to look and sense, "Does it look like it's resonant in their body?" If it's only in their head, it's not going to happen. If you don't sense any resonance, you say, *"You know, it sounds important to me but, as you speak it, I'm trying to sense where it actually lives in your body."* Again, until the words starts awakening something in the body and the rest of the nervous system, they are just words.

And, in terms of what we are calling the "COACH field," this does not only mean that it needs to be resonant for the client. It has to be resonant in your body as the coach as well. We like to say to our clients, *"If I can't feel it, probably nobody else is going to feel it. I'm really easy. I'm just trying to open myself to feel whatever it is that you really want. I want you to touch me with what you are up to."*

We will say, *"Until you can touch at least one other person with your dream, it's not going to come true."* That is one of the things you do as a generative coach. You are representing the community and the world at large. We point out to the client that, "It won't come into the world until you touch people." As Steve Jobs claimed, *"If you dream alone, you stay a dreamer. If you dream with others, you change the world."* That is why you have to be able to touch others with your dream.

Once clients can verbalize their intention positively, succinctly and resonantly, they need to envision it. *There should be a color image that goes with the words.* Sometimes these will come spontaneously. Other times, we will ask, *"What would be a visual image that goes with those words?"* The visual images can be metaphorical images or they can be social reality images, like a literal picture. It can be good to have both. If everything is just dolphins and angels, it becomes a little ungrounded in classical reality. On the other hand, if the client says, *"I see myself sitting in a chair and saying this and doing that"*, the potential for much creativity disappears. So, its nice to get both a dreamer image and a more realistic image of the intention.

Finally, *the client has to embody the intention*. Until it comes through their body, it's just an interesting idea. There is an insightful proverb from Papua New Guinea that states, *"Knowledge is only a rumor until it is in the muscle."* In Generative Coaching we adapt that to say, *"An intention is just an empty wish until it is in the muscle."*

So, we will say to the client, *"If you ask your body to make a movement that represents your intention, can you show me what it would look like? What is the somatic model that goes with your words and images?"*

Expressing intention

In summary, we help the client translate the intention into a simple three-part statement. We talk a little informally with them about what they want and then get a good COACH connection. And then we ask the client to say, at least a couple of times, this three-part statement:

1. *What I most want to create in my life is* ... (Five words maximum.)

2. *And if I were to sense an image that goes with that, it would be . . .*

3. *And if my body were to make a movement that represents my intention, it would be . . .*

As generative coach, you are dropping in the question and seeing what words, image and movement would come out. One of the ways you know you have a good COACH field is that the answers come spontaneously to the client. They don't have to figure out the answer. It comes. And frequently it's even a surprise. A client says: *"I don't know why this is coming, but it is this* (word/image/gesture)". So, you let it emerge. And in a generative state it will. You don't have to do anything to make it come. It just emerges.

The following steps constitute one of our basic prototypes for expressing an intention in generative coaching.

1. Settle in, settle down

2. Open a COACH field and bring attention to the client's intention

3. Client speaks:

    –What I most want to create in my life is (verbal statement)

    –The image that goes with that is _____

    –And the somatic model of that is (show movement)

4. Coach takes time to receive and absorb each statement, then feeds back:

    –I hear that what you want to create is (repeat verbal statement)

    –And the images that go with that are (feed back images)

    –And a somatic model of that is (feed back movement)

    –And I send you much, much support for that!

5. Coach invites the client to repeat process 3-4 times, with same or different content.

Demonstration of Expressing Intention

The following is a transcript from a coaching session Steve did in one of our programs in which, after establishing a COACH state with the client, he guides the client through the process of setting an intention.

Steve: *Let's explore your intention for this session. So, there are three statements that I want to invite you to make and move through slowly and carefully, just noting what each word touches; what it awakens. The first one is, "What I most want to create in my life is..."*

Client: *What I most want to create in my life is... a sense of inner peace.*

Steve: *Let's just breathe with that. Awesome. "Inner peace." Then the second statement is "If I allow a visual image to come that goes with that, it might be . . ."*

Client: *I get an image of waves just coming up onto a shore with the sun going down. There is a beautiful orange light just shimmering on the wave after wave just coming up the shore and just fading away. And the next wave coming into itself is just as beautiful. There is just wave upon wave.*

Steve: *That's awesome. So, a beautiful color image of the waves and the shore, and the orange.*

Client: *A golden orange and sun going down in the distance, and just this beautiful shimmering light.*

Steve: *Okay. Let's let go of the words and just breathe that up and down your spine. You don't want too many words because you don't want to get caught in the head, but use the words to name the image and then let the image take you wherever. Maybe you can be looking at me for this last statement. Say, "If I let my body make a simple movement that represents that intention, maybe it would be . . ." and I also invite you to actually speak the statement out loud.*

A SENSE OF INNER PEACE

Client: *What I'd most like to create in my life is the state of inner peace. And that movement that goes with that would be...* (Makes a rhythmic gesture with both arms up and down in front of his body.)

Steve: *That's cool. Welcome. Welcome.*

So, saying something verbally out loud is a way to bring your imagination out into the outer world. And you can do this by yourself, which I encourage clients to do as a morning practice or before a big performance. Speak your intentions out loud. Then, come back to resting state.

That's great. How about we try one more time? This time we see just see what comes up new this time. It could be the old statement but often it's a little bit different. So, "What I most want to create is . . ." And I just invite you to look here. (Gestures to the space between the two of them.)

Client: *What I most want to create is . . . humor.*

Steve: *That's interesting. So, you also want to create humor. And, again, if you tune in to the visual part of your river and follow that thread of "I want humor, I want peace," what visual image would come with that?*

Client: *Interesting. A very powerful image of the Buddha's smile.*

Steve: *Oh, the Buddha's smile. Cool. Let's just welcome that Buddha's smile. That's awesome.*

And "If I let my body make a movement that goes with that . . ."

Client: (Makes a rhythmic circular gesture with both arms moving away from and then back towards his body.)

Steve: *That's good. Let's just breathe with that. It really feels like you're touching some really important things for this next part of your journey. Peace, living with peace, living with humor, sunset, the water, the Buddha, that movement. Welcome. Just notice how your mind can begin to gather all those words and images into a beautiful constellation that begins to become visible in the world. Welcome. Welcome. Welcome. Are there any simple vows or commitments you want to take from this experience?*

Client: *Yes. What I intend to do is to take this and include this beautiful imagery and this lovely feeling as part of my daily practices and make sure I practice this so that it becomes my default state.*

Steve: *I send you lots and lots of support for that.*

Client: *Thank you.*

An important thing to note about this demonstration is the steps that Steve took to keep the client connected to the generative relational field between himself and the client. Steve's comment "Maybe you can be looking at me for this last statement" and his gesture to the space between the two of them serve to keep the client from becoming isolated into his own personal map of the world and stay connected to the generative potential in the coaching relationship.

Varying Your Approach to Fit the Client

Sometimes clients will struggle to get the words for their intention first. So, the coach might just ask, "Well, do you have a picture?" Or the coach might say, "Show me your somatic model first." Frequently we find that people "can't quite get a picture" and we'll say, "Well, show me your intention with your body." They will do that and then they say, "Oh, I just saw it. I see the picture now."

So, even though we might typically start with words, follow with the image and finish with the somatic model, it is not a rigid order. For some people, their body is going to speak first, and then they can find those simple words. Some people are naturally more verbal, others more visual and others are more somatic. As a generative coach, we can adapt to their needs and thinking styles.

Demonstration of Varying Your Approach to Fit the Client

The following is a transcript from a coaching session Robert did in one of our programs in which, after establishing a COACH field, he guided a client through a variation of expressing intention.

Robert: *So, what is your intention? What is something that would be really important for you to create?*

Client: *I've been playing around with this idea over the past few days, which is to create and help manifest a creative environment.*

Robert: *To help manifest a creative environment. Is there a particular area of your life or a certain context where it would be important to do this?*

Client: *Professionally. Either building teams or creating the right situation for teams to innovate.*

CREATIVE ENVIRONMENT

Robert: *As you say that, partly just because of my own personal interest, I find that notion of manifesting a creative environment very exciting. I get a feeling like, "Oh yes, okay. This sounds really great." How fully does that resonate with you when you say "manifest a creative environment?"*

Client: *I also get really excited. (Smiles broadly.)*

Robert: *And it seems pretty succinct.*

Client: *Yeah, it's deliberately succinct so it can work at various different levels. Helping to communicate more effectively between one or two people, or within a group, and within a team.*

Robert: *Great. And do you have any particular image that goes with this intention?*

Client: *I hadn't really been thinking about an image previously, actually. I've had a sensation of a color. There'd been a cool blue feeling to it. It's being quite nebulous, there's no distinct image.*

Robert: *Actually, sometimes I find that images get clearer when you make a somatic gesture first. I noticed that you spontaneously made a few gestures while you were talking. Do you have a specific gesture and movement for your intention to help manifest a creative environment?*

Client: *Yes, it is something like this* (hands and arms gesturing out from the body). *It is kind of like throwing a lot of Legos unto the floor* (laughs) *which is a perfect sort of metaphor for "We're going to build something and create the right environment."*

Robert: *Well, there's sort of an image there, isn't there?*

Client: *Yeah, but yes (laughs) that's an image, you're right.*

Robert: *I love that. Okay, so like "throw these Legos on the floor." And maybe there's also a way that something blue goes with that. I don't know.*

Client: *(Laughs) Yeah, and so it's kind of a light blue feel to the room which helps me maintain the COACH state I think.*

Robert: *Awesome.*

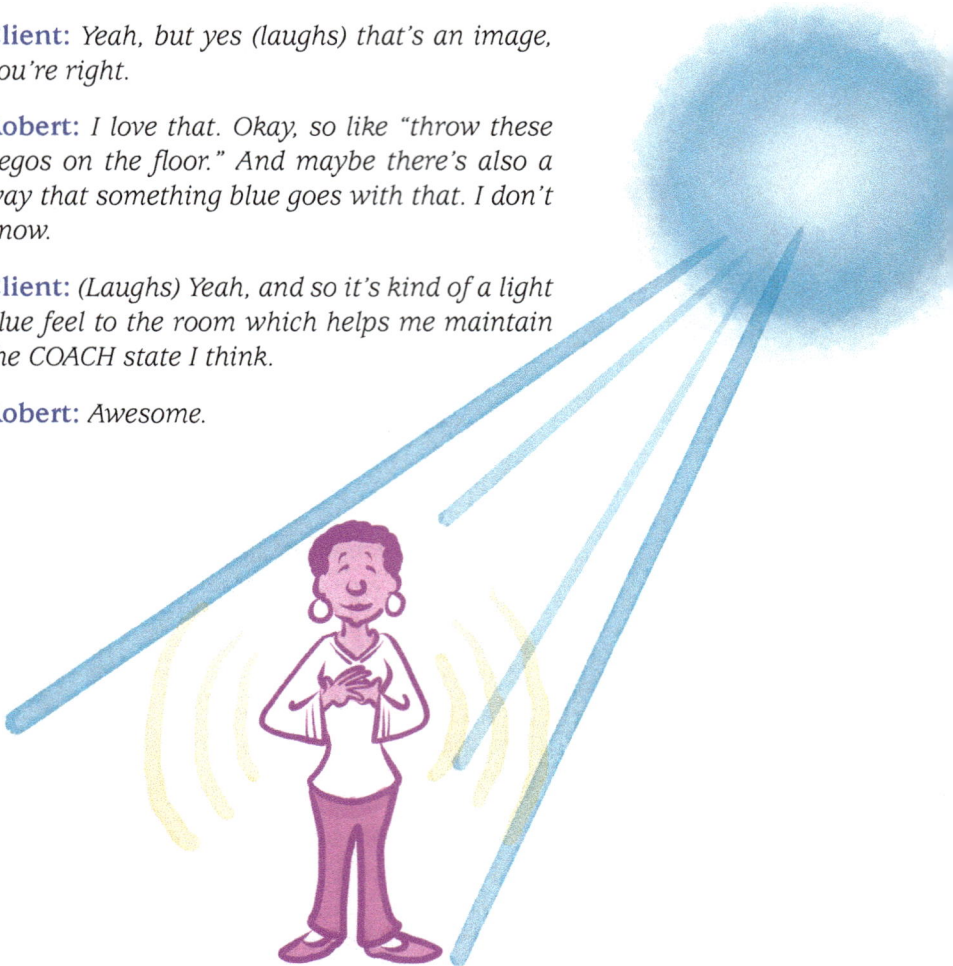

In summary, step 2 is essentially about opening to the quantum field of infinite possibilities, and then choosing one of those possibilities that most resonates with your heart and your body as well as your head. In Generative Coaching, we do that in a very robust way rather than just through some intellectual, verbally-based approach. We want the client to be able to say it simply, feel it, see it and show it with their body. If they don't have an intention that really resonates in their body, in their vision, and in simple words, then they may be connected to possibilities but none of them are going to get actualized.

The next part of the coaching process, step 3, is about gathering the resources needed to begin to bring the intention into concrete action.

CREATIVE ENVIRONMENT

The Variable

Remember to sit with yourself daily
and sink into states
you do not know how to bind,
thoughts you cannot package
and send off to others,
moments you cannot dress up
and take out for the day.

Take time to walk out of step
and step out of time;
to squeeze yourself
through that narrow space
between questions and answers
into the abyss we call life
where, even if for and instant,
everything is possible;

then spread that feeling like marmalade
across your life.
Let it sweeten your day.
Let it be the variable
in the equation of your habits
that orchestrates little surprises
every now and then
just enough to remind you
that there is always more that you know

– Nick LeForce

Chapter 5

Step 3
Establishing a Generative State

The third step in the Generative Coaching process is to establish a high quality creative performance state. The goal of this step is to develop and sustain creative consciousness at optimal levels. Once you've got clarity about the direction you want to move by defining your intention in step 2, the next question is, "How do you organize your state so that you can move into action and stay in a sustained high performance state?"

This involves finding the answer to such questions as, *"How to stay focused on your desired state and not become distracted? How to have a centered mind-body presence? How to stay connected to supportive and empowering resources, both inner and outer?*

The Three Positive Connections

Whatever life brings you on your path to fulfilling your intention, you want to meet it and move through it with a sustained, creative, high-performance state. A primary prototype for how to get into this state involves simultaneously holding three connections: 1) to yourself and to your deepest somatic center – your source; 2) to the intention that you want to bring into your life; and 3) to what we call your "field of positive resources," which includes both physical things in the environment but also non-physical energetic types of resources (e.g., mentors, role models, family members, ancestors, friends, places in nature, pets, spiritual or historical beings, etc.).

These three connections produce a very powerful creative state. The significance of this state is one of the key contributions of the generative change work.

When you can truly and strongly hold these three connections simultaneously, new thoughts and ideas will begin to emerge naturally and spontaneously. Things will begin to come to you and through you. You do not have to consciously or cognitively try to make them come or figure them out.

This is the essence of "generativity." Something new emerges naturally from the field created by the three connections to yourself and your source, your positive future intention, and your bigger field of resources.

Your intention

Your center

Your field of resources

The three positive connections

Establishing the Three Positive Connections

The following steps summarize our basic prototype for developing a generative state through the three positive connections.

1. Open a COACH field

2. Develop the three positive connections:

   - **Positive intention** (words, image and somatic model) *What do you most want to create in your life?*

   - **Mind-body center** (experience of presence and commitment) *Where do you most deeply feel the connection to that intention in your body?*

   - **Positive resources** (mentors, models, family, friends, places, memories, spiritual or historical beings, etc.) *What connections would best help you achieve your goal?*

3. Use self-scaling to optimize intensity levels of each connection to at least 7 out of 10 or more.

4. Holding the integrated sense of the three positive connections, begin to work towards the intention.

Demonstration of Establishing the Three Positive Connections

The following is a transcript from a coaching session Steve did in one of our programs in which he is guiding a client to enter a generative performance state following the basic prototype.

Stephen: *Hi! Now we're on our first date together.* (Laughter) *So, I am just wondering now, while we are up here, is there one thing that would be really great for you to be able to achieve or accomplish in your life? What would that be at the top of the list?*

Client: *Should I say it out loud?*

Stephen: *Please, yes. If it's okay.*

Client: *There is a business project that I want to develop to really big scale.*

Stephen: *Super. And if you really successfully achieved the goal in that business project, what would be the outcome?*

Client: *I would feel joy and calm, safe and that I brought something into this world, and when I leave this world there would be something left behind other than bones.*

Stephen: *Awesome. And what would you have actually achieved? Would it be creating a certain company, or creating a product, or is it to be able to make a contribution to people in the community?*

Client: *It's more about a community that has a common view of things and that is united by the idea of seeing things in a similar way.*

Stephen: *I wonder if you can represent it in terms of visual image. Would that be people standing around holding hands? Would they be doing something together?*

Client: *Yes, it resembles what is happening here, with lots of people and I am kind of on the stage.*

Stephen: *Cool. If we were thinking in terms of a time, would that be in a month, in 6 months, in a year, in two years?*

Client: *In two years.*

Stephen: *Super. So really tune into the sense that "over the next two years, I really want to do everything I can to create this positive community." And when you get to the end of these two years, what would be your somatic model for "I did it"!*

Client: (Smiles and raises both arms over his head in a triumphant gesture.) *Yes!*

Stephen: (Mirrors the movement.) *Do it again a couple of times.*

Client: (Repeatedly raises both hands over his head in a triumphant gesture.) *Yes! Yes! YES!*

Stephen: (Mirroring the movement.) *Great! Maybe we could try just a very sort of slow sense so that you could feel that "Wow. I did it" inside. And really sense it.*

Client: (Slowly raises both hands over his head in a triumphant gesture.)

Stephen: (Mirroring the movement more slowly.) *Any images that go with that?*

Client: *It's more like sounds. Applause, cheering*

Stephen: *Awesome! Yeah! Cool. On the scale of one to ten, how important is that feeling to you in terms of your life path to be able to create something like that?*

Client: *It is a big project and seems a bit daunting. I would say about six.*

Stephen: *Six. Good to know. And can you just sense and let me know where you feel that most deeply in your body.*

Client: *Here.* (Points to the area just below his diaphragm.)

Stephen: *So, there is something here* (points to the area just below the diaphragm) *that really wants to come out. Awesome. So, this would be your center. If you start getting too much up here* (gestures to upper chest and head), *you probably won't get very far. But you can really feel this deep passion "I really want to make difference to the world" in the center of your body.*

Client: *That's correct.*

Stephen: *So one way to reinforce and deepen this first positive connection is to repeat your somatic model of commitment, "I am going to create this positive community."*

Client: (Raises both arms over his head in a triumphant gesture.)

Stephen: (Mirrors the movement.) *Try that a few more times. This is the magic.*

Client: (Enthusiastically raises both arms over his head several times.)

Stephen: (Mirrors the movement.) *That's cool! And on the scale of 1 to 10. how much do you feel that now?*

Client: *Now it is 10.*

Stephen: *Awesome. To get into a generative state, it is sort of like holding a bow and arrow. One part of you is focused to the future intention and the other part is grounded in your body in the present. So, as you make the connection to your intention, feel the deepest place of connection in your body. Make the commitment to the intention and, at the same time, connect with your center. It might be located here* (points to diaphragm area) *or lower. Just sense where.*

Client: (Keeps arms extended but lowers them in front of his chest.)

Stephen: (Mirrors the movement.) *Great, and then hold that, hold that and now say:" And I connect to my center."*

Client: *And I feel the connection to my center.*

Stephen: *Now, feel the connection to the intention and the connection to your center. This is another one of those conversational dualities. "I go towards my intention and I go down and stay connected to my center."*

Client: (Pumps his fists in front of his chest.) *YES!*

Stephen: *He is ready to go. Get out of his way!*

Client: (Pumps his fists in front of his chest.) *Yes! Yes! Yes!*

Stephen: *Okay, then, let's do one more thing – the third connection. To do this very important journey, hold the question, "Who can I call upon for support?" Who would be a good resource that really gives you the support, the knowledge, the confidence, that you can do that? These could be family members, ancestors, historical figures, phenomena from nature, places, etc.*

Client: *My family*

Stephen: *Your present family?*

Client: *Yes. Especially my wife.*

Stephen: *And may I ask you your wife's name?*

Client: *Kirsten.*

Stephen: *Great. Let's welcome Kirsten and imagine she heard your voice calling "Kirsten!" Just sense where in this space around you is there the presence of Kirsten. Could be here ....or ....here.* (Gestures to various places around the client's body.)

Client: *A bit behind my back at the right.*

Stephen: *What would she be saying or doing?*

Client: *She would say; "I believe in you. You can do it."* (Crosses hands over his heart.)

Stephen: *"I believe in you."* (Mirrors the gesture.) *Awesome. And just feel her presence. I can see that there is more of a softness that comes into your body when you do that. And on the scale from 1 to 10 how much can you feel her presence?*

Client: *Nine.*

Stephen: *Super. Holding these three connections will put you into superior performance state. A core principle of Generative Change is, "Don't ask yourself to perform until you've created the conditions for success." And these three connections are the fundamental conditions for success. So, one more time, the first step is connecting to your intention. Say: "I will!" And find the somatic model.*

Client: *I will! (Raises both arms over his head in a triumphant gesture.)*

Stephen: *Okay. And then the second step, "I connect equally to my center. The more I go into the world, the more I drop into my center."*

Client: (Lowers his arms and pumps his fists in front of his chest.) *Yes!*

Stephen: *And as I connect to my center, I open myself to the support from my field of resources. I feel my wife's presence and her message, "I believe in you."*

Client: *(Crosses hands over his heart.)*

Stephen: *And when you have those three connections, you are truly ready to move into action.*

Client: *Yes! I feel fully confident that I can do it.*

Stephen: *And I send you my full support.*

Establishing
the three positive connections

1) ASK THE
CLIENT FOR
WHAT THEY
WANT

2) CREATE A
GENERATIVE
FIELD TOGETHER

CLAP
CLAP YEAH!
CLAP

I BELIEVE IN YOU

YES!
YES!
YES!

3) FIRST CONNECTION: THE INTENTION

3) THIRD CONNECTION: THE FIELD OF RESOURCES

2) SECOND CONNECTION: THE CENTER

Tracking the Three Positive Connections

Once the three positive connections have been established, it is important to continually track the strength of the connections with respect to one another. As we pointed out earlier, a coaching session always has two levels:

1. **the content of the work**, and

2. **the context** (the underlying state of the filters within which the work is performed).

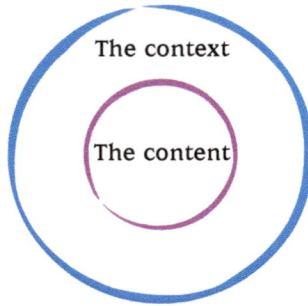

A good generative coach constantly tracks both levels, giving priority to the state of the filters. Whenever the filters that are holding the content start going into some type of CRASH state, all "performance work" needs to be paused until a COACH state can be re-established. Thus, a main responsibility of a generative coach is to develop, monitor, and maintain a COACH state, and the three positive connections, in both the client and in himself or herself. The quality of the COACH state and the three positive connections will directly determine the quality of creativity achieved in the session.

If the strength of any of the three positive connections drops below 7 out of 10 during a coaching session, the level of generativity and performance will decrease dramatically.

In the previous demonstration, Steve used the analogy of holding and aiming a bow and arrow. There is a type of creative tension that emerges from the relation between the counterbalancing forces of one hand aiming the arrow toward the target and the other pulling the bowstring toward yourself. The level of that creative tension adjusts depending upon the direction and distance of your target. This is like the counterbalancing forces of moving into the world with your intention and feeling the connection to your center at the same time. When you can create that balance and add the connection to your resources, it opens a type of safe sphere around you.

In order to create and maintain that balance in a Generative Coaching session, it is important to keep the following points in mind:

* The three positive **connections can fluctuate** along a continuum

* **Focusing** on one connection can diminish the connection to the other connections

* **Self-scaling** is a very simple and helpful tool for tracking and optimizing the connections through time

* To remain in a generative state, the **level of connection** needs to be at least 7 out of 10 or above

* Self-scaling can be used any time, anywhere to **calibrate** the level of the connections

* In generative coaching sessions, it is used intermittently to **gauge and shift intensity** levels

There are three basic ways to increase any of the connections:

1. language

2. visual images

3. somatic modeling.

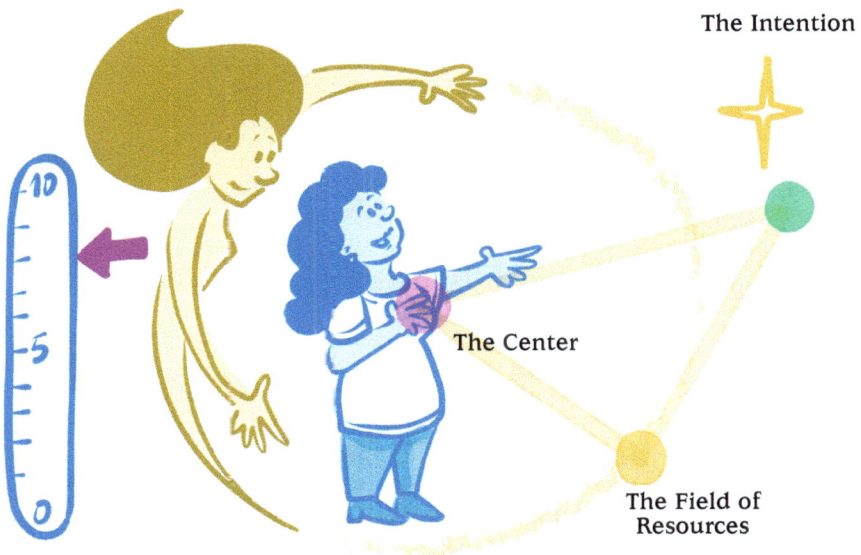

The Intention

The Center

The Field of Resources

Demonstration of Tracking the Three Positive Connections

The following is a transcript from a coaching session Robert did in one of our programs to help a client use self-scaling and somatic modeling to establish and sustain the three positive connections.

Robert: *I'm very pleased to share this time with you, and I'm sure that we can do something magical in this session. And what I'd like to do, before we start even thinking about what it is that you'd like to work on, is to take a few moments and get into COACH State. I get the sense that right now your energy is a little bit higher up here.* (Gestures to upper chest and head.) *So, if we just both took a breath and tuned into a place in ourselves that is deep enough that it's always spacious and safe. Just connecting into that place, breathing into that place, feeling that breath spread like a warmth through the body. When you do that, what do you experience?*

Client: *A sense of calm.*

Robert: *Yes, and anywhere in particular? Is it all through the body or is there a place where you most notice that calm?*

Client: *It is all around me.*

Robert: *All around? Yes. Interesting. And I see a little more sparkle coming to your eyes. And also, I sense more presence here in our connection together. It's nice to connect around this calm place.*

Client: *Yes.*

Robert: *Great. On a scale of 0-10, how strong would you say your sense of connection to that calm resourceful place is right now?*

Client: *I'd say it's sort of fluctuating between a 6 and a 7.*

Robert: *Between 6 and 7. Good to know. What do you think could help you stabilize it at 7 or more?*

Client: *Relaxing my neck and shoulders* (moves upper body) *and feeling the ground beneath my feet.*

Robert: *What happens when you do that?*

Client: *It becomes stronger, like 8 out of 10. And I can open up more.* (Smiles.)

Robert: *Yes. And I see more playful energy starts to come out. Ready to play?*

Client: *Ready to play.*

Robert: *What would be something that would be really interesting for you that you would want to create more in your own life?*

Client: *I want to create more of a sense of openness, and for that openness to be present more of the time.*

Robert: *Are there particular places where that would be especially important to have that openness? What is a context that would be especially important for you?*

Client: *The place that comes to mind is at work.*

Robert: *OK. At work. So let's see if we can get this into a statement of 5 words. What would be your simple way of stating that?*

Client: *I want to create a more spontaneous place of openness at work.*

Robert: *Great. Actually, that feels pretty solid to me – "What I really want to create is a more spontaneous place of openness at work." When you say that, does it resonate in your body? What happens inside of you when you say it?*

Client: *Have a slight panic that I'm not going to be able to.*

Robert: *We like to say that, usually within 5 seconds of when you actually state a real intention, the other side comes out. And it makes sense. So that slight panic is going to be a team member. I just want to say to that panic, "Welcome. Welcome to the team." When you do that, what happens?*

Client: *Welcome.* (Relaxes and smiles.)

Robert: *Yes. I see a little more of your sparkle comes back. Great. So, yes, there's naturally this concern, "Am I going to be able to?" Yet, you also still really want to have this more spontaneous place of openness at work.*

Client: *Yes.* (Speaking firmly) *That is what I really want.*

Robert: *Do you have an image for what that would be like?*

Client: *I do. The image is a place of light, a place of gentle breeze, blues, and greens, blue skies, and big skies, open expanse.*

Robert: *Yes. So here it's certainly not a literal image of your work environment. It seems more an image of what that spontaneous openness feels like – this big expanse, blue sky.*

Client: *Yes. Blue sky.*

Robert: *A lot of openness. And what would be your gesture for this intention? "What I really want to create at work is . . ."*

Client: (Moves arms in a circular motion.) *I go around the circle. And I'm flowy.*

Robert: (Mirrors the movement.) *Cool. I like the flowy part. So, let's put all three together. So you're going to say the 5 words, "I really want to create . . ." and see that picture and make the gesture.*

Client: *What I really most want to create is a spontaneous sense of openness at work.* (Moves arms in a circular motion.)

Robert: *I noticed your voice kind of trailed off a little bit at the end when you said "at work." How strongly right now do you feel connected to that intention, committed to that intention?*

Client: *I'm committed to creating a spontaneous sense of openness. And I think I get many more things coming in because actually, I want to have it in many other places as well.*

Robert: *So you really want to create more of this sense of spontaneous openness in your life. Work being a key area.*

Client: *Yes, so what I most want to create is a spontaneous sense of openness at work and in my life. In my life!* (Moves arms enthusiastically in a circular motion._

Robert: *Yes.* (Mirrors the movement.) *Great. How strongly do you feel your connection to that right now?*

Client: *When I said that I had warmth that just came through my whole body.*

Robert: *That's good to know. That's a good calibration. On scale of 0-10, what would you say the level of connection to that would be?*

Client: *9. Yes, definitely 9.*

Robert: *Good. Now the second question is, as you have that 9 connection there, how strongly do you still feel connected with yourself and your center?*

Client: *I think I probably disconnected a little bit.*

Robert: *That's good to know. So let's just take a moment and bring attention to both your intention and your center. What do you need to do to stay a little bit more connected to yourself? What gesture could help you with that?*

Client: (Makes circular movement with arms towards the body.) *I just need to bring them together a little bit more.*

Robert: (Mirrors the movement.) *Yes, that makes sense.*

Client: (Breathes deeply and smiles.) *I'm here.*

Robert: *Okay, great. "I'm here. And I know what I want." What I'm going to invite you to do now is to go to the third connection. So the question here is, in order to be more spontaneously open at work ~ and in your life ~ you're going to need a connection to resources that can help you and support you in order to have that spontaneous openness. If you were to hold these two connections to yourself and your intention and then open to this bigger field of resources, who or what comes to you that can actually be a support to you and really make sure that this happens? You don't have to try to think or figure it out. Holding these two connections, just let something come.*

Client: *So what came was a very quiet voice. I don't know who the voice belongs to but it was a really quiet voice. And sometimes that voice isn't heard because it's so quiet, so nobody hears it.* (Makes circular gestures around her ears with her hands.)

Robert: *Yes. So let's take a moment and breathe with that. And I see that there's something happening with your hands.* (Mirrors the movement._ *So let's just pause a moment. I think it was Emerson who said, "Let us be silent so that we may hear the whispers of the gods." So, let's take a moment and say to this voice, "Welcome."*

Client: *Welcome.*

Robert: *Yes.*

Client: *It's really fascinating because the voice wants to be welcomed in. And has lots to say. But is not often heard.*

Robert: *Yes.*

Client: *It's here.* (Gestures near her ears with her hands.)

Robert: *Yes. It's here.* (Mirrors the movement.) *Right here. And what we want to do is make sure the connection to this voice is strong. If you think about it right now, 0-10, what is your level of connection to this voice?*

Client: *Around 8.*

Robert: *How do you know that it's 8?*

Client: *Because the voice feels close. I can actually feel it. It is almost like a real softness of space and it's almost tangible. It isn't solid, but it occupies the space.*

Robert: *Awesome. So let's take a moment and let's test all three of those connections right now. I have this voice. I have my intention, "What I want is really to create more of this spontaneous openness in my work and my life." And then I have that connection to myself. To really make this happen, I've got to stay committed and I've*

got to listen. I've got to stay connected. So right now if you were to test your connection to all three of these – your intention, yourself and this soft voice – what would you say is the level of connection?

Client: *It takes some work.*

Robert: *It takes more than that. It takes practice.*

Client: *It's really so hard.*

Robert: *And that's why you have a coach. Let's explore something. What would be your somatic model and movement for this generative state where you can actually stay connected to your intention, yourself and that soft voice? What would that movement be like?*

Client: (Moves arms in a circular motion, then makes a circular gesture with arms towards the body and finally up towards her ears. Continues silently making this pattern several times.)

Robert: *Yes.* (Mirrors the movement.) *That's it.*

Client: (Takes a deep breath and smiles broadly.) *The voice came inside.*

Robert: *Yes. How about your connection to yourself?*

Client: *Oh yes. Okay. Now we're all going.* (Continues to enthusiastically make the pattern of movement.)

Robert: *Wow. That's a great voice tone. When you speak, it seems to be coming from deep in your body.*

Client: *Absolutely! Right from here.* (Points to her solar plexus.)

Robert: *Yes, yes. Our next step is to get ready to move into action holding all of those three.*

Client: *I'm quite fine. I'm already off! It's fine.* (Continues to enthusiastically make the pattern of movement.)

Robert: *Okay?*

Client: *Oh yes, now I am.*

Robert: *I believe you.*

Client: *Thank you. Oh, it's great!* (Smiles broadly.)

We want to point out again the significance in generative coaching of joining clients in their gestures and somatic models. This was an important part of both of the demonstrations presented in this chapter. Mirroring the client's movements serves to strengthen both the somatic intelligence and the field intelligence between coach and client.

The vehicle for creative change is not the coach and it's not the client, it's the conversational space that you're sharing together. So, the coach is trying to find that and surrender to it and be supported and guided by that. And then his or her individual professional actions are coming out of that "we" space.

It is also useful to notice how the first two steps are setting up the third step. The first step is all about the connection to my center through the COACH state. The second step is about defining and connecting to my intention. In step three, we're holding both of them and adding the connection to the additional resources we need to reach that intention.

Once a strong generative state has been established, it is time to go to step 4 and move into action!

Tracking
the three positive connections

2) CONNECT
TO THE
CENTER

1) GET INTO
COACH STATE

A MORE
SPONTANEOUS
PLACE OF
OPENNESS
AT WORK AND
IN MY LIFE!

3) CONNECT
TO THE
INTENTION

10
9
8
7
6
5
4
3
2
1
0

4) CONNECT TO THE FIELD OF RESOURCES

WELCOME

5) WELCOME AND ACKNOWLEDGE ANY OBJECTION

The Door

Go and open the door.
Maybe outside there's a tree
or a wood,
a garden,
or a magic city.

Go and open the door.
Perhaps outside
there is a dog rummaging.
Maybe you'll see a face,
or an eye,
or a picture of a picture.

Go and open the door.
If there's a fog
it will clear.

Go and open the door.
Even if there's only
the singing darkness,
even if there's only
the wind's hollow breath,
even if
there is absolutely nothing there,
Go and open the door.

At least
there'll be
a breeze.

~ Miroslav Holub

Chapter 6

Step 4
Moving to Action

Step four of the Generative Change process is to begin to move into action. This where the Generative Coaching process becomes really focused on bringing the intention into a concrete expression – moving from the quantum field to classical reality. The important focus at this step is to how to translate a dream into a concrete expression. Thus, the goal of step four is to develop and actualize plans, using feedback to adjust and refine the movement towards reaching the intention. This involves breaking the whole into its parts, and then assembling the parts into a sequence or "critical path."

At step four, we're at the place where we can say, *"Okay. Let's do it. Stay focused on the necessary actions. Just keep moving. Keep stepping forward into the world."* The goal of the coach is to support the client and keep him or her focused on the actions necessary to reach the desired state.

The questions to be answered at step four include, *"What are going to be the key actions necessary to manifest your intention? What is the critical path? How do you create a path that has both concrete clarity and yet has enough flexibility to stay generative and to stay open to be aware of opportunities you had not anticipated and make corrections?"*

To answer these questions, you need to start putting things on a timeline and making a "storyboard." You're defining both the key actions and the feedback that you're going to need in order to bring your vision and your intention into action. Two of the key processes we frequently like to use for step four in Generative Coaching are "imagineering" and "storyboarding."

Imagineering a Path to Success

Imagineering is a term coined by Walt Disney to describe the process he used to form dreams and then turn them into realities. A powerful insight into the imagineering process is provided by one of Disney's co-workers who pointed out, *". . . there were actually three different Walts: the dreamer, the realist, and the spoiler. You never knew which one was coming into your meeting."* Imagineering involves the coordination of these three subprocesses: Dreamer, Realist and Critic, all of which are necessary to move from an intention into effective action.

The Realist makes a choice and creates a plan to achieve one of those possibilities.

The Dreamer opens the field of possibilities.

The Critic makes suggestions to make the plan even better.

Coordinating Dreamer, Realist and Critic

The **Dreamer** is necessary to form new ideas and goals. The **Realist** is required in order to transform ideas into concrete expressions. The **Critic** is crucial in order to evaluate, filter and refine the steps into something that is both effective and ecological.

A Dreamer without a Realist cannot turn ideas into tangible expressions. A Critic and a Dreamer without a Realist just become stuck in a perpetual conflict. A Dreamer and a Realist might create things, but they might not reach the necessary level of excellence without a Critic. The Critic helps to evaluate and refine the creative path.

In summary:

* A Dreamer without a Realist and Critic is just that: only a Dreamer.

* A Realist without a Dreamer and Critic is a Robot.

* A Critic without a Dreamer and a Realist is a Spoiler.

* A Dreamer and a Realist without a Critic are a research & development department – they make a lot of prototypes but lack the quality standards for success.

* A Realist and a Critic without a Dreamer are a Bureaucracy.

* A Dreamer and a Critic without a Realist are a roller coaster of Manic-Depression.

The Dreamer opens new possibilities

The Realist transforms them into reality

The Critic improves the result

Imagineering Questions

Thus, the processes of imagineering can be associated with three particular areas of questioning: **(1) the "dreamer"** (where the whole and parts of a vision are generated), **(2) the "realist"** (where the dream is translated into a concrete structure), and **(3) the "critic"** (where the concrete expression of the intention is relentlessly improved). One way a generative coach can support his or her clients to realize their intentions in a wise and balanced manner is to be sure that the clients have clear answers to each of these areas of questions. The following is a summary of the fundamental questions required to effectively "imagineer" a positive intention into a concrete expression.

Dreamer:

* *What is your positive intention?*
* *What is the larger purpose of that intention?*
* *What are the potential benefits to yourself and others (family, friends, colleagues, etc.)?*
* *What other possibilities could the intention lead to in the future?*

Realist:

* *What is the time frame for reaching your intention?*
* *Who are the key actors in achieving your intention?*
* *What are the specific next steps necessary to make progress?*
* *What is evidence or feedback that you are making progress?*
* *What resources are available to assist in the success of reaching your intention?*

Critic:

* *What is missing from your current plan?*
* *Who might be positively or negatively affected by the achievement of your intention?*
* *Why might someone object to your reaching your intention?*
* *What are their needs or expectations?*
* *What do you need to refine, modify or change about the plan?*

"Storyboarding" the Steps to Putting the Intention into Action

Storyboarding is a process for defining such a path that was also developed by Walt Disney. Disney's primary imagineering strategy, and his major strength as a realist, was the ability to chunk and sequence his dreams into pieces of a manageable size. Disney was the innovator of the process of storyboarding (a process now used by all major film developers).

A storyboard is like a visual table of contents – it is a set of still images (literal or symbolic) that represent the crucial sequence of events needed to move from some present situation to a desired outcome. An effective PowerPoint presentation, for example, is a form of storyboard. The "storyboarding" process is a very powerful way of organizing and planning that can be particularly useful for helping a client create a path to achieve their intention.

To assist a client to make a storyboard for achieving a particular intention, you would guide him or her through the imagineering questions presented earlier – focusing especially the "realist" questions – and then help the client explore how he or she could organize those answers into a sequence of steps.

The following is an example of a type of storyboard, showing a possible path from intention to realization.

Set intention	Open to possibilities	Transform inner critic
Get external support	Connect with resources	Celebrate key successes

Putting the Storyboard on a Physical Timeline

In our Generative Coaching work, it is important for us to engage the client's somatic mind in the storyboarding process. One way that we do this is to use a physical "timeline" in order to help the client identify and sequence the steps to reach their intention.

To make a physical timeline, we are essentially transforming space into time. We have the client imagine a line on the floor in which a particular point represents the present and one direction indicates the future, while the other indicates the past.

We then invite the client to step onto the line at a point representing the present and to face in the direction of the future and enter the COACH state. For the *"dreamer"* phase of the process, we ask the client to orient their attention to the future direction on the timeline and to review or to recreate their positive intention from step 2 of our 6-step model (in the form of five words, an image and a somatic model). We then establish the three connections necessary for the generative state (their somatic center, the future intention and their field of positive resources).

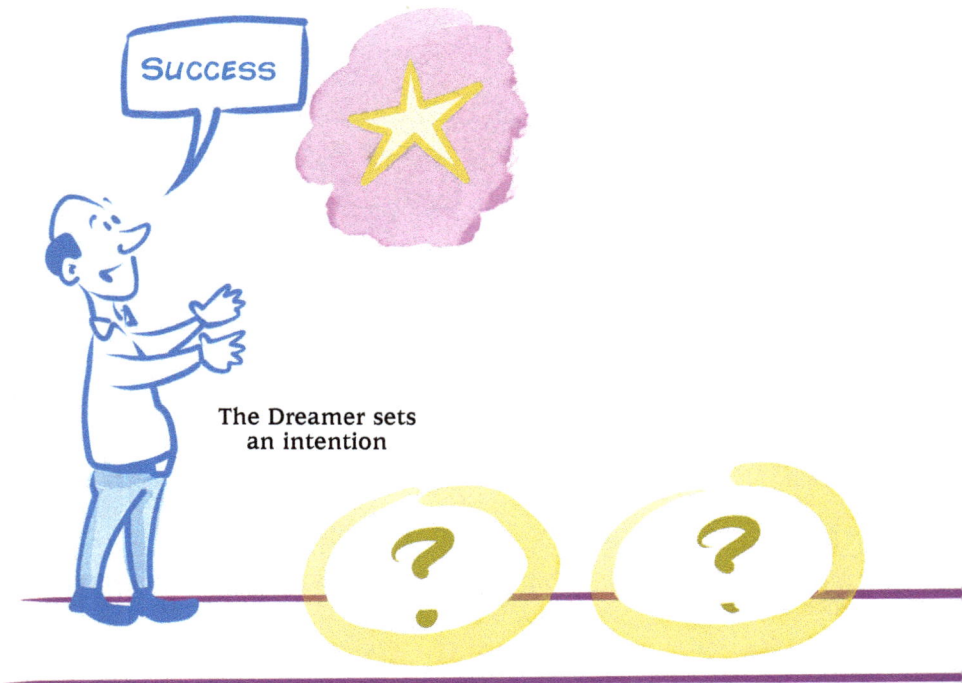

SUCCESS

The Dreamer sets
an intention

Reminding the client to continue holding these three connections, we instruct them to walk up the timeline in the direction of the future to a point in representing the achievement of their intention. We make sure that he or she can really see, hear and feel what the achievement of the intention will be like.

We are then ready to enter the *"realist"* phase of the process and move into action. Having the client return to the "present" position on their timeline, we ask the client to imagine 5-7 locations along the timeline in between the present state and the desired state of achieving their intention. These locations indicate the key action steps needed to reach the intention.

Making sure that the client is in their generative state, we next invite the client to step into the first location. Using images, words and somatic models, the client engages his or her creative unconscious to explore what needs to happen at this first step in order to move in the direction of the intention.

Then, moving slowly up the timeline, we repeat this process for each location on the timeline until the client has reached the location, indicating the fulfillment of their intention. By the time the client has reached the desired state, they should have a good sense of the key steps, or storyboard, needed to reach their intention.

YES!

The Realist creates steps to move into action

The COACH holds the space

Chunking Down the Storyboard

At first, we ask the client to just focus on the "big chunks" or major steps that will be necessary to move from the present state to the desired state. We then want to continue refining the storyboard through the process of "chunking down."

Chunking down involves breaking something into successively smaller pieces in order to manifest it. For example, to write this book, we had to chunk the book into chapters, the chapters into topics, the topics into key points, the key points into sentences, the sentences into words, the words into syllables and those syllables ultimately into letters.

Similarly, helping a client move into action involves "chunking" his or her intention into a storyboard, and then chunking the storyboard down into successively more detailed steps. This is typically done by focusing on each of the main steps in the storyboard and asking the question, *"What, specifically, has to be done in order to achieve this step?"* Once again, the answer to this question is explored in the form of images, words and somatic models.

Doing this will help to clarify each of the main steps and define the sequence of specific goals necessary in order to accomplish that step.

The same chunking down process can then be repeated for each of the specific goals, defining the successive actions that will be necessary to achieve the specific goals.

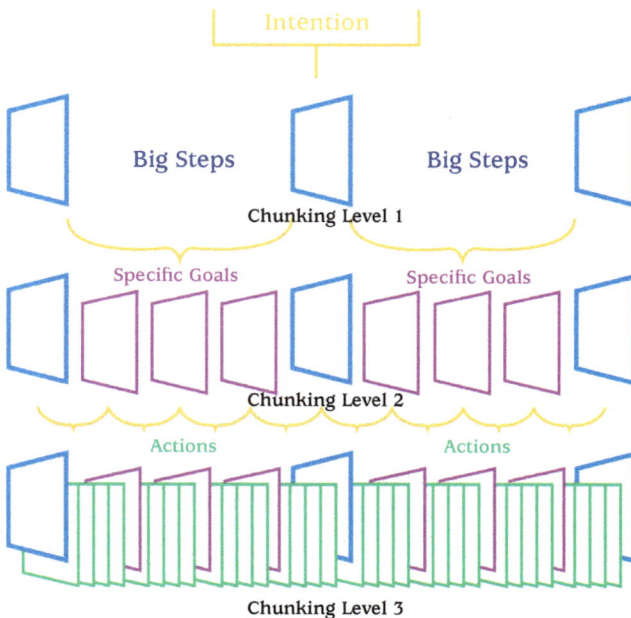

Intention

Big Steps   Big Steps

Chunking Level 1

Specific Goals   Specific Goals

Chunking Level 2

Actions   Actions

Chunking Level 3

This is the same type of process that all productive people follow in order to realize their dreams and intentions. Such an approach helps to keep everything in perspective and not *"lose sight of the forest because of the trees."* This process is forever in elaboration, revision, refinement, and transformation. Thus, it requires the creative mindfulness of the COACH state and the three connections of the generative state to guide it.

We can summarize the prototypic storyboarding process in the following basic steps:

1. Lay out a **physical timeline** extending from present to desired state.

2. Begin in **COACH state** and define or reconnect with the positive intention.

3. Establish the **3 points of connection** for the generative state (somatic center, intention and field of resources).

4. Physically move to the **desired state** in the future on the timeline.

5. Lay out **5-7 locations** representing the basic path from the present to the desired state

6. Step in first location and **use images, words and somatic models** to engage the creative unconscious and explore what needs to happen at this step.

7. Move slowly to the second location, finding new somatic models, images and words.

8. **Move through each location** on the timeline until the storyboard is complete.

9. Slowly walk through the timeline several times, each time **chunking down** and specifying the steps.

Demonstration of Creating a Storyboard

The following is a transcript from a coaching session Steve did in one of our programs in which he is guiding a client through the steps of beginning to create a storyboard.

Steve: *It's always a good start to a session to say, "First things first. Let me find a way to get a positive connection with myself." Do you have any good practices for that?*

Client: *Just breathing.*

Steve: *So, if it would be okay, you can coach me and teach me what it would be like to use that method.*

Client: *Just nice, deep breathing, in through the nose, out through the mouth and breathing right down into the belly.*

Steve: *So, let's slow down so that you can feel the connection to the heart, to the belly. Take a few moments to have that deep breathing through the nose, feel it settle down and start thinking how low can you go to feel your energy go deep back into the earth.* (Makes a movement with his hands as if pushing down toward the Earth.)

Client: (Mirrors the movement.) *That's tree roots.*

Steve: *It's sort of an interesting process, how low can you go. What happens when you do that?*

Client: *It's really relaxing, the movement.* (Repeats the movement.)

Steve: *Great. So, this would be our baseline COACH state, if you will. And probably along the path, we'll need to just pause and come back to something like this, to reconnect with that baseline, get back to just that simple connection. What would you say is your level of COACH state on a scale of 1 to 10 at this point?*

Client: *I would say 8.*

Steve: *Super. So, our next step is, "What would you most like to create in your life?"*

Client: *I would like to create wealth in my life.*

Steve: *How much wealth are we talking about?*

Client: *Infinite.* (Makes a wide open gesture with her hands and laughs.)

Steve: *"I want money!"* (Laughs.) *That's the somatic model for that.* (Mirrors the gesture.) *It looks good on you. No, really, it actually touches me to hear you talk from that place. You're both relaxed and you feel abundant, open, and at ease. I couldn't help but notice that your body really went through a shift as you expressed "I want to create wealth."*

Client: *I'm opening out to the possibility. I also feel a bit guilty, like I shouldn't say that in front of all these people. It seems greedy.*

Steve: *But I could see that it's not greed. That you are really speaking from there* (points to heart).

Client: *Yes. You're right. I can feel it in my heart.*

Steve: *Yes. If we can just take a few minutes and drop into the intelligence of your body. Something in you really wants to create a life that has wealth and all the different experiential associations to that. I'd like to suggest that we use that connection to just do a first dry run of a storyboard. Not really focusing on the details, but saying, "I'm really stepping in to a commitment to open my life to this place and living in a much bigger, happier way."*

Client: *No more smallness.*

Steve: *No more smallness. Super. And what I'm going to invite you to do is get that connection to your heart and take the first step on your timeline.*

Client: (Starts to move on time line. Breath shallows and jaw tenses.)

Steve*: Aha, you see this?* (Points to the head and jaw.) *Every client has telltale signs of CRASH. So, you see that and you want to point out to her that this is one of hers. So, this* (points to jaw) *is where the cut off to her primary creativity is one of the telltale signs. I need to see that as the coach because if she goes through the timeline like this* (clenches jaw), *it'll just be a bunch of inauthentic stuff and then her critic will beat her up afterwards. This is usually where the critical anger is, in the locked jaw here.*

So, if you connect to your heart, at this point in your life you want to say, "No, I don't want to live from what I should be or what I can't be. I want to live for what my most passionate dream is." Do I have that right?

Client: *Yes.*

Steve: *Good to know. So again, I'm just going to remind you as your coach, if you try to make it happen here* (points to head and jaw), *you'll end up in the critical ditch. If you listen to here* (points to heart), *it will guide you each step of the way.*

Client: (Takes a deep breath, touches her heart and makes an open gesture outward.)

Steve: *Wow. When you come from that space, I just feel beautiful energy like, wow, this is really one of your main gifts.*

Client: *My jaw feels nice and relaxed.*

Steve: *If you can stay connected with that place in your heart and hold the question of how to really create this state of happy wealth, what would the first step be?*

Client: (Steps forward on the time line and gestures outward from her heart.) *Open up to the possibilities.*

Steve: *Open up to the possibilities. And then what if you thought in terms of opening the possibilities of the specific thing that you could do in your everyday life, what would it be? What would be a specific action you could do in your everyday life that would begin to translate infinite possibilities into, "I'm doing it, I'm walking, I'm creating it, I'm living it."*

Client: (Gestures outward from her heart.) *Start the process of selling my business.*

Steve: (Mirrors the gesture.) *Selling your business. Super. That's a pretty big one. Let's just pause and feel that decision, that commitment, feels like it's touching many different levels of your life.*

Client: *It's like letting go of "the child."*

Steve: *Yes. When I tune to that with you I feel this sort of quiet, openness. Also a deep seriousness, a calm seriousness.*

Client: *Definitely.*

Steve: *Super. So in terms of chunking, what are the steps that you would need to take in order to do that?*

Client: (Steps forward on the timeline and gestures outward from her heart.) *The next step is realizing I'm not in love with my current business anymore. And connecting to the excitement of a new direction.*

Steve: *So just take another small step towards that excitement and ask yourself, "What would be some of the simple things that might be next to do?"*

Client: (Steps forward on the timeline and gestures outward from her heart.) *Qualify in Generative Coaching.*

Steve: *Take the step, sister.*

Client: (Steps forward on the timeline and gestures outward from her heart.) *Get my website up.*

Steve: *Got it.*

Client: (Steps forward on the timeline and gestures outward from her heart.) *Convince my husband that I'm selling the business.*

Steve: *That sounds like another big one that goes along with that first step. Let's pause there and really make sure you are connected to your heart.*

Client: *It feels very real.*

Steve: *Awesome. So again, we're looking to create the conditions to explore these places that have been off limits; "I can't really go into my dreams." As you now occupy the space as a professional coach, dipping into whole new territory ~ how you would carry yourself, how you would conduct yourself, how you would be presenting yourself ~ let's go into the specific steps. This is not a one-time exploration, but as you go through a career change, it's a daily practice which you engage in order to open to the new self-image and to new behavior. I have to recognize, "I've been kept out of this territory through my conditioned CRASH responses. I need to open into that new territory and specific actions, and ask myself, 'What do I actually do?'"*

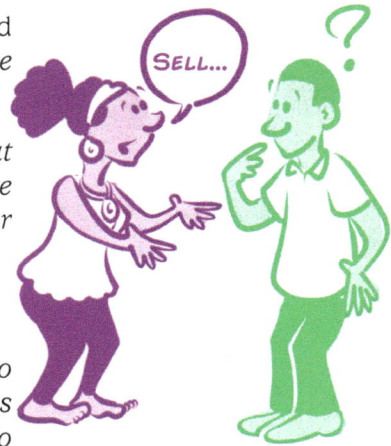

Client: *Write the content for my website. I've already started doing some coaching and joined your organization so that I can get officially accredited.*

Steve: *Well done. I really mean that. Welcome to a community that really supports your professional development. So that feels to me like that's probably about all we can put in the storyboard for now. If we were to add more pieces, it would probably be too much.*

Client: (Laughs.) *Too many chunks.*

Steve: *Yeah. Nice to know that and to laugh about it.*

So getting ready to sell the business and having a conversation about that with your husband, sounds like an important part of your storyboard, and then stepping into how to create a new professional identity. So what I'd like to suggest is that we just lay that out on the timeline again, in a way that you can be practicing this on a daily basis for a number of weeks – as a way to begin to sort and reorganize how you recreate yourself. So, how about we go through the steps again? (Invites the client back to the beginning of the storyboard.)

Client: (Steps forward on the timeline and gestures outward from her heart.) *So I've got a slipped disc in my neck, which means I have to stay on reception and not do so many treatments on clients. Our current business is beauty therapy. So I have the time to start writing content for my new website and making the plans to build the site. I can simultaneously make the plans for selling my existing business as well. So this slipped disk, which is incredibly painful, is actually a gift.*

Steve: *Yes. It often is a message. So, if we put that into the storyboard, the narrative opens up an even deeper level of creative language.*

Client: (Takes a deep breath and smiles.) *Yes, it's like I'm being given permission and allowing myself to do the preparation.*

Steve: *You look beautiful in that state. How many of you feel that? So that's what we want to be coaching her to do. Connect to that. Don't trust yourself to move until you feel that.*

So then there's the step of "what I do to let go of the old business." That has many parts including a conversation with your husband.

Client: *I have an ex-employee who will buy it without hesitation, I hope. She's expressed a lot of interest.*

Steve: *Yes. Okay. Now the next step, and that conversation with your husband. So let's stay connected to that place in your heart and step there.*

Client: (Steps forward on the timeline and gestures outward from her heart.) *It has to do with his fear of letting go as well. And that's scaring me, because this business actually has been our baby.*

Steve: *Got it. "So letting go of the business, dealing with the fears, with me, with my husband."*

Client: *And the sadness.*

Steve: *And the sadness. Let's welcome that and hold it in your COACH state. Remember those tree roots you talked about when we first started.*

Client: (Makes a movement with her hands as if pushing down toward the Earth. Takes a deep breath and relaxes.)

Steve: *Great. That's right. Come back home to your true source.* (Gestures towards her heart.) *"All my life I tried to figure out what I wanted using only my head. Now I have to live from deeper down. And then I step into my new professional identity again. Completing my coaching training and getting accredited, these are all the sub level pieces that I would need to be focusing on in terms of translating the dream into reality."*

Client: *Very practical.*

Steve: *Yes, very practical and then that allows you to find yourself in that future state.*

Client: (Steps forward on the timeline and makes an open gesture outward from her heart.) *It opens the space out and I can welcome it in.*

Steve: *And then that place of "I did it!" What would be that state of "I did it?"*

Client: (Raises arms triumphantly above her head and smiles broadly.)

Steve: *As I said at the beginning, I sincerely send you deep support for a beautiful, important path that you're attuned to for you and for your gift to the world. How many of you send support to her?*

(Applause)

Client: *Thank you.*

Creating a storyboard

GET INTO
COACH STATE

SET AN
INTENTION

CREATE STEPS
TO MOVE INTO
ACTION

CERTIFICATE
GENERATIVE
COACHING

WEBSITE:

ACKNOWLEDGE
AND
TRANSFORM
OBSTACLES

PROJECT
YOURSELF INTO
THE FUTURE
STATE

As we can see from this demonstration, a storyboard is not simply an abstract, intellectual plan. It is a "story" that includes the challenges, characters and emotional reactions related to the creative journey of change. This is because Generative Change is not simply about improving or refining an existing behavior. It often involves transformation or evolution at an identity level.

In this demonstration, Steve helped his client to chunk down the general intention of "creating wealth" into the process of making a career change. This involved her opening to an expanded understanding of "wealth" and letting go of an old identity in order to embrace a new dream that was more aligned with her heart. As Steve pointed out, this frequently involves exploring new territories that have previously been "off limits."

Committing to a path that is aligned with our deepest intention also begins to bring out the *"critic"* and the inevitable obstacles. In this case, the client's husband was a potential *"critic"* who could object to the plan. She also had her own *"inner critic"* who felt guilty and greedy for wanting more from her life. These are the places that we will bring more attention to at step 5. The key during the storyboarding process is to meet each step with our COACH state and the three positive connections: our center, our intention and our resources.

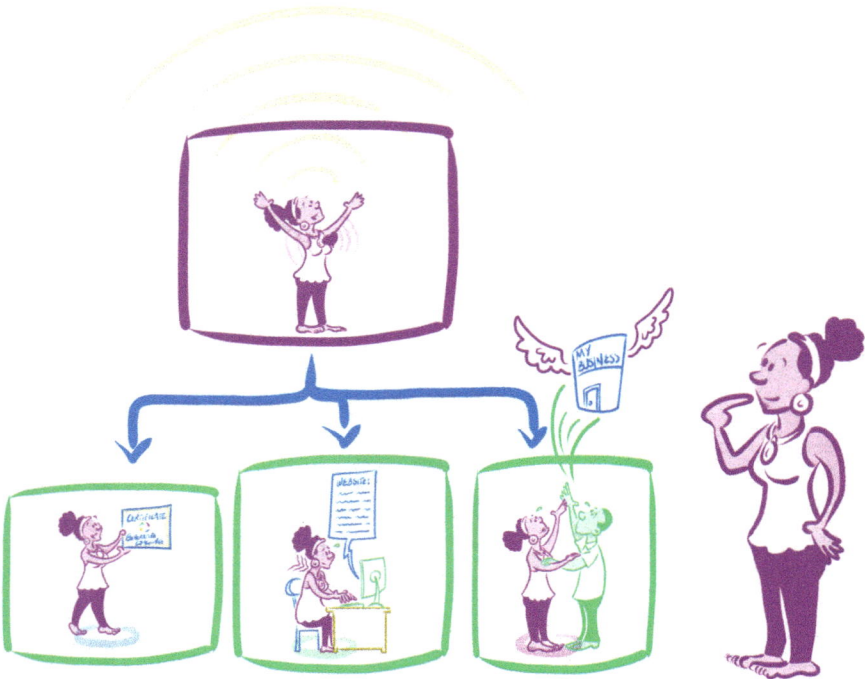

Making a "Deep Structure Storyboard"

Another form of chunking involves moving from more symbolic and metaphorical representations to literal reality. When we are working with Generative Change at the level of deep structure (such as a shift in identity), it is difficult to initially define in concrete, literal terms what exactly is going to happen. Deeper structures have many, many possible expressions when they eventually reach the level of surface structure. Thus, storyboarding the process of change at the level of deep structure is often more easily done through symbols and metaphors, which can then begin to be chunked down into actual concrete actions.

Demonstration of Making a "Deep Structure Storyboard"

The following is a transcript from a coaching session Robert did in one of our programs in which he is working with a client to initially make a deep structure change that will eventually be expressed in terms of social reality.

Robert: *Hello. Pleased to meet you. Before we get started, I would like to invite us to make four movements and four suggestions together. The first one is* **"slow down."** *So we just make the gesture "Slow down." And as we make the gesture, we slow down the inner dialogue, we slow down the breath, the heart. And as we slow down, it allows us to bring a deeper awareness to the holon of the body. When I slow down, I like to make sure, can I feel my tailbone, can I feel my knees, my ankles, my wrists, my nose, my ears? So, I really want to slow down to be aware of my entire being.*

Slow Down

And the second gesture and suggestion is **"pause."** *And pause means to be silent and still for a moment. And that allows me to really connect. So I pause to not only be aware, but also connect to my heart, my belly, my eyes, me ears, my nose, all the way to my feet and through my feet to the Earth. And then connect through the top of my head to the sky and the stars. So, in that pause I connect.*

Pause

The third suggestion and the third gesture is to "breathe." And in this breathing I am drawing energy into my body from the air and the Earth, and I am also opening the heart, opening the mind, opening the shoulders.

And the fourth suggestion and the fourth gesture is to "center"; especially center in the belly.

And then I kind of check. On the scale of zero to ten, where is my COACH state right now? And I am curious what number would come to you.

Breathe

Client: *Nine.*

Robert: *Great. I can feel that nine. I can see a lot of difference in your body from when we started. Welcome. I see you. And now that we've set these signals, if we need them as we start moving into action, either one of us can use them. At some moment I might say, "OK, let's pause." Or I might say, "Let's breathe." Or, "Let's center." And you could too, if you need to pause or breathe. Okay? Make sense?*

Center

Client: *Yes.*

Robert: *Our next step is about your intention. I am curious what are those five words that you have found for your intention.*

Client: *I want to realize my depth.*

Robert: *That's a place where I would like to pause (makes pause gesture). And let's really breathe those words through. I heard you said them, but they were pretty fast. So, if you were really to bring those words down into the belly, "What I most want to create in my life is … to realize my depth."*

Client: *My real desire is I want to meet the real me.*

Robert: *Ah, that's interesting. And notice the way the head says the intention is more abstract – "realize my depth." And the words from this deeper place are, "I want to meet the real me." And I just want you to know that when I hear and see you say that, I want to meet the real you too. And I am curious, as you say that, and you let the words resonate here, what's the image that comes to you?*

Client: *I see an angel and the radiant light all around him, glowing.*

Robert: *That's interesting. Let's say, "welcome" to that angel. I am curious: is there a gesture that goes when you say those words "I want to meet the real me" and see that angel?*

Client: (Folds her arms around herself.) *I want to embrace myself.*

Robert: *Fantastic. So, welcome.*

So, the next question is about something we can put on your timeline so that we can start to create your storyboard. Is there a certain context in your life where that would be really important or maybe where you would find it challenging right now to meet your real self? It could be in a personal relationship or at work, or . . .? Where would you most like to really have this connection with your real self?

Client: *In my work.*

Robert: *In your work. Here is where it would be interesting to go up your timeline to some time in the future where you are able to be fully connected with your real self at work. What seems to be a good time frame for that? Would it be next month or six months where you could really feel this? What would be a realistic time frame for you to really become yourself fully at work?*

Client: *Like a year.*

Robert: *A year. Great, that makes sense to me. So, that's our first movement to realist mode. We say, "A goal is a dream on a timeline." If I don't put the dream on a timeline, it stays a dream. If I keep saying, "some day," I'm just a dreamer. But when I say "one year," now that dream has suddenly become a goal. If you don't put it in time, it's not a goal. So, this is a very important first step for the realist. Let's walk to that place a year from now on your time line. And we really want to get a strong sense of that desired state. And just let your body move up that timeline to where you spontaneously feel, "This is about a year."*

Client: (Client takes several steps on her timeline and stops.)

Robert: *Great, and as you really take a moment and put yourself here in your future, in the context of work, see what you see, hear what you hear, feel what you feel. How do you know "Yes! I really have made that deep connection with my real self and can bring it here in my work." What do you notice? What are the things that you notice most are different or changed? Maybe it's what you see, or feel, or say, or do. What's the most important to you?*

Client: *My inner feelings changed. I widened and became more of myself. Back there* (points to the present on the timeline) *I was like a drop, but here in my future I am like the ocean.*

Robert: *Awesome. The poet Rumi had a beautiful saying. "You are not a drop in the ocean. You are the entire ocean in a drop." So, you are a drop that becomes the ocean. Would that involve a change in the gesture for your intention? What would be your somatic model of "I am now at work and I am the ocean"?*

Client: (Moves arms out in a wide circular gesture that returns to her body. Smiles broadly.) *I wish to embrace the whole world.*

Robert: *Ah, that's interesting. So, back there* (points to "present" on time line) *I am embracing myself and here in my future I want to embrace the world. And I see such a big smile. Let's do that again.*

Client: *(Repeats the gesture and smiles broadly.)*

Robert: (Mirrors the gesture.) *Fantastic. Great. How strongly do you feel your commitment to this intention? Zero to ten.*

Client: *Ten.*

Robert: *Ten. And where in your body do you most sense that commitment?*

Client: *It's here.* (Gestures to her heart.)

Robert: *Fantastic. Okay, so now we are going to come back to the present on your timeline.* (Robert and client return to the beginning of the timeline.) *And we stay connected to your intention "meet the real me at work" and the image of the angel, the drop becoming the ocean and that gesture of embracing the world.*

Client: (Moves arms out in a wide circular gesture that returns to her body.)

Robert: *And as you stand here in the present how strongly do you feel the positive connection to your somatic center.*

Client: *Nine*

Robert: *Great. So we have these two connections: my intention and my somatic center. Now we want to get the third connection. As you think about this journey to really become this ocean at work, who or what from your bigger field of resources are you going to need most to support you?*

Client: *It's my son.*

Robert: *Your son. What's his name?*

Client: *Alex.*

Robert: *Where would you feel Alex if you were to bring his presence here?*

Client: *Here.* (Gestures to her left side.)

Robert: *And right now. Zero to ten, how strong do you feel the connection to Alex?*

Client: (Smiles broadly.) *Ten.*

Robert: *Ten. I see that. Hi there Alex! Welcome.*

So, if you were to take the first step from here toward that desired state a year from now, what would that step be? And we have to be careful. We don't want to go up into the head for the answer. We want to stay with this deeper intelligence. (Moves arms out in a circular gesture that returns to his body). *Just take the step and see what emerges. If you took that first step what would you do? What may come to you could be something very practical, concrete and literal. It might also be more symbolic or metaphoric. It might come in words or images. I am curious what comes to you as a first step on this journey.*

Client: (Takes a step and moves arms out in a circular gesture that returns to her body.) *The first thing is that I have to have courage to look inside myself.*

Robert: *So, let's pause.* (Makes pause gesture.) *Slow down. Really breathe that in.* (Mirrors the client's gesture.) *And I just want to say that it really feels resonant and right to me: the courage to really look inside. And, as we breathe that through, I am curious: what is the image that comes to you?*

Client: *I see the door opening.*

Robert: *The door opening.*

Client: *These are big doors and a hall, a giant corridor that is really magnificent and beautifully decorated. It's really beautiful.*

Robert: *And what is your gesture for this courage to open the door.*

Client: (Opens arms out from the body as if boldly pushing doors open and takes a step forward.) *Like that.* (Smiles broadly.)

Robert: *I see that you already stepped through the door. What would happen next?*

Client: *It's strange, but there is an ocean there.*

Robert: *An ocean there? That's interesting. And, by the way, it's always a good sign when you say "It's strange." It means it's not coming from your cognitive mind. So, this ocean comes. And what does that represent for you?*

Client: *I am surprised because I thought the ocean would be there.* (Points to the future state on the timeline.)

Robert: *So, what does it mean that the ocean is here? What would you do with the ocean? Do you put your foot in it? Do you swim in it? Do you drink it? Or what?*

Client: *To swim.* (Makes a swimming motion with her arms.) *To swim.*

Robert: *Interesting. To swim.* (Mirrors the swimming motion.) *So, as you swim, what happens next?*

Client: *I need a pause.* (Brings her arms to her sides.)

Robert: *Fantastic.* (Brings his arms to his sides.) *So, I am curious. You say: "Pause" What happens here? What is it that you pause for?*

Client: *I want to enjoy the moment. To live it through.* (Smiles broadly.)

Robert: *Let's pause and breathe that through your body. "I want to enjoy the moment." So, courage is important, but also enjoyment. Because courage with no enjoyment, what's the use? Joy without courage, it not going to go anywhere. So, as you enjoy this moment, what happens? What comes for you?*

Client: *I do not have any thoughts, I just feel calm, safe and confident.*

Robert: *Calm, safe and confident. So, we have courage, joy, calm, safe and confident. And does an image come with it?*

Client: *Clouds. I know that I can lay down on them but I do not fall through them. They hold me. They lift me.*

Robert: *What's your somatic model for that? Enjoying in that place, feeling safe and confident.*

Client: (Hesitates for a moment and then extends her arms out in front of her as if holding a child.)

Robert: *Let's breathe with that for a moment. I say that because I noticed that there was a little bit of CRASH for a moment. So let's breathe with that and repeat the gesture.* (Extends his arms out in front of him as if holding a child.)

Client: (Extends her arms out in front of her as if holding a child.)

Robert: *And I really want you to take your time with this. Remember, your intention is about getting really more profound, really getting to meet all of yourself.*

Client: *I want to open my heart in this way.* (Extends her arms out in front of her as if holding a child.)

Robert: *Let's do that slowly.* (Mirrors the gesture slowly.)

Client: (Slowly makes the gesture.) *To open and not to close again. To keep it open.*

Robert: *I can understand why there might be some CRASH with that. One thing is to open the door. It's another thing to really open your heart. If you were really going to open your heart, especially at work, what resources would you need? Make sure Alex is here with you.*

Client: *It's freedom. It's like wind. It comes around any obstacles and nothing can stop the wind.* (Moves her arms in a wavelike motion in front of her.)

Robert: (Mirrors the movement.) *An unstoppable wind.*

Client: *It can move freely and change its direction.* (Repeats the wavelike movement and begins to make a noise like the wind.) *Whoooo whoo…*

Robert: *I am an auditory person. I am always happy when a sound comes. Image, feelings, words, that's good. But sound is really great!* (Mirrors the movement.) *Whoooo whoo…*

Client: *And it just goes far, far away forwards.*

Robert: *Good. Fantastic. When you say that and do that, I have shivers all over me. So, now, we're almost ready for our next step. So, let's just review the storyboard so far. "I have my intention, my center and Alex, and the first step: Take the courage to open the door."* (Opens arms out from has body as if pushing doors open.)

Client: (Mirrors the gesture.) *And then swim.* [Makes a swimming motion with her arms.] *And then the clouds.* (Extends her arms out in front of her as if holding a child.) *And then the wind.* (Makes a wavelike movement.) *Whoooo whoo…*

Robert: *And then what happens?*

Client: *I cannot be stopped.*

Robert: *I believe you. Where do you go?*

Client: *I don't want to stop. I want to move forward.*

Robert: *So, remember we had this place in your work world. So, if you bring your wind to work, one year from now what will happen at work with that wind?*

Client: (Moves hands from her belly to her throat and then gestures out like a fountain.) *There will be a sense of freedom, and I will be able to speak out freely and openly.*

Robert: (Mirrors the gesture.) *Let's pause. There is something very important here. "I would have a voice. I would speak freely and*

openly." And let this voice come through, especially through your throat. "I can speak freely and openly at work." (Repeats the gesture.) What happens with you when you connect with that?

Client: *The wind transformed itself. It changed its form. It's like a pipe, like a hurricane. But it doesn't destroy anything. It goes freely. And it is easily transformed.*

Robert: *Well, it's a powerful voice you have – when you speak from yourself. Then what happens? What do you want to do then?*

Client: *I feel more relaxed in my body. And calmness and some kind of basic trust that everything will be okay.*

Robert: *It's very interesting. They say that in the center of the hurricane it is always calm.*

Client: *It's really calm inside. There is no wind inside. The wind is outside.*

Robert: *That's interesting.*

So, we have this very symbolic and metaphoric storyboard here, which is in many ways appropriate for identity level change. Ultimately, we will explore how to express it in specific actions and specific contexts. But what is most important for now is to really get this storyboard in the muscle.

When you build a storyboard like this, in Generative Coaching, it's the kind of thing that also starts to enter your dreams. It becomes so much a part of you. You don't have to wonder, "What was my storyboard again?" It is your guiding path. So, let's just walk that one more time, when you are ready.

Client: (Moving to the beginning of the timeline.) *I begin by embracing myself like this* (folds her arms around herself.) *Then I take the courage to open the door, like this* (opens arms out from the body as if boldly pushing doors open and takes a step forward.) *Then I swim in the ocean* (makes a swimming motion). *Then I pause and rest in the clouds* (extends her arms out in front of her as if holding a child). *And then I am free like the unstoppable wind* (makes a wavelike movement with her arms) *Whoooo whoo…And that turns into hurricane.* (Moves hands from her belly to her throat and then gestures out like fountain.)

Robert: *And what happens?*

Client: *I understand that I need to have more courage in my work. I know how to do a lot of interesting things but I do not tell people about them. I started to think that some things are worth saying. For example, I can help people heal. I work with coaches, psychologists, and trainers. I help them to widen their potential. I work with difficult cases. People come to me who seem to have no way out and I help them. For example, I helped one girl who was told she was infertile to get pregnant and give birth to a child.*

Robert: *Thank you sincerely for sharing all of that. It sounds to me that you have a big gift to bring to the world and have decided to "open the door." It is nice to know more about the real you.*

This is an interesting illustration, by the way, of how chunking works. We started with symbolic images and gestures. Now, the storyboard is starting to become literal. You are showing the courage to talk about these things right now. And that's why we say this work is "generative." We don't start by planning, "Well, I'm going to say this. I'm going to say that." But when I gather

the right resources, I will spontaneously say the right things at the right time.

I just would like to say, I send you my full support and, as Milton Erickson used to say to us, "If you need it, my voice will go with you to remind you." But I might not say the words. It might just say "Whooo whoo . . ."

(Applause.)

Client: *Thank you so much for that.*

Robert: *Any final words that you want to say to your fellow classmates?*

Client: *I really want to open myself to people and help others. And if what I am doing resonates with any of you, I really would love to connect with you, because I really enjoy what I am doing and would love to share it.*

Robert: *Thank you. This is why Stephen and I started the IAGC. To have a generative community and share our resources with one another. Welcome to that community. How many of you send support to her?*

(Applause.)

Client: Thank you.

Making a deep structure storyboad

IMAGE OF INTENTION: TRANSFORMING FROM A DROP INTO THE OCEAN

KNOW THY SELF

INTENTION: TO MEET MY REAL SELF

OPENING THE DOOR

SWIMMING IN THE OCEAN

EVERY STEP IN THE STORYBOARD IS EXPRESSED IN WORDS, IN A SYMBOLIC IMAGE AND WITH A SOMATIC MODEL

WHOoo

WHooo

WHOOOoo

PAUSE: ENJOYING THE MOMENT

BECOMING THE UNSTOPPABLE WIND

FREEING MY VOICE

ANTONIO MEZA

The type of storyboard Robert helped his client make in this demonstration is what we would call a "deep structure storyboard." It is more about an inner journey that must take place before it can be transformed into actual concrete behavioral expressions. The client's intention to "realize her depth" and "meet her real self" is about an identity shift rather than a specific behavioral objective. When we make a shift at an identity level, many specific behaviors will begin to change, as we witnessed beginning to happen in the demonstration,

Using a Daily Diary as a Way to Get Feedback

As both of the demonstrations illustrate, the process of moving into action requires constant elaboration, revision and refinement. Thus, it is important to continually use feedback to optimize the storyboard. To support this, we will sometimes ask the client to keep a daily diary and reflection upon:

* Which behaviors/thoughts/actions supported your intention?

* Which behaviors/thoughts/actions took you away from your progress toward achieving your intention?

The client may then use that information in order to know what adjustments to make to his or her storyboard. A simple recipe to help a client make use of the feedback from his or her daily diary is to determine: *"Which behaviors that do not help will I let go of? Which behaviors will I do more of?"*

Engaging the "Critic" to Refine the Storyboard

The process of getting feedback naturally begins to engage the "critic" mindset. Feedback obviously relates to "critic" questions such as *"What is missing from your current plan?"* and *"What do you need to refine, modify or change about the plan?"*

Beginning to explore other critic questions like, *"Which behaviors/ thoughts/actions took me away from realizing my intention?"* and *"Which behaviors that do not help will I let go of?"* will by their nature lead us into step five of the Generative Coaching process – Transforming Obstacles.

Similarly, critic questions such as, *"Who might be positively or nega- tively affected by the achievement of your intention? Why might someone object to your reaching your intention?"* And *"What are their needs or expectations?"* will lead us to identify and confront significant obstacles and interferences that will need to be addressed and transformed.

In the next chapter, we will explore how we address these issues and challenges in Generative Coaching.

Move into action by projecting your intention into the future and then using the "Dreamer, the Realist and the Critic" to support you to make it a reality.

The World

The world marches on
whether or not
you march with it.

The world gives
its all to you
regardless of your
readiness for it.

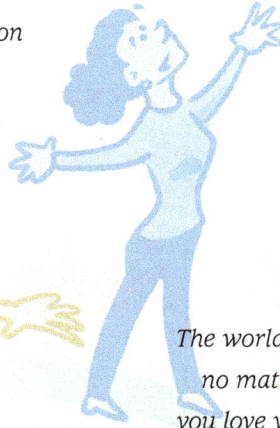

The world completes you,
no matter how much
you love your limitations,
and gives back to you
what you reject.

The world offers too much
to the wary,
hides too much
for the fearful,
demands too much
of the shy,
and takes too much
from the stingy.

The world is a harvest
for the bold
and a hell
for the self-righteous.

The world is a prison for those
who try to escape from it
and a paradise for those
who fall in love with it.

The world turns
with you even when
you turn away
from the world.

You choose
whether the world
is your friend
or your foe
because the world
is a burden when
you try to carry it
and a blessing when
you let it carry you.

~ Nick LeForce

Chapter 7

Step 5
Transforming Obstacles

The fifth step of the Generative Coaching process is about what to do when you encounter the inevitable interferences and obstacles that you will meet on your creative path. In Generative Coaching, we say, "The more interesting a life that you want to have, and the more success that you want to create in the world, the bigger the 'demons' that you're going to attract."

This may sound cynical, but we actually take a basic positive attitude towards obstacles and resistances. We say that the obstacles, the problems and the failures are essential integral parts of any sort of creative success. Based on the work of our mutual mentor Milton Erickson and practices like Aikido, we look to see how we can actually welcome the obstacles. We then explore how we can creatively engage with an obstacle to transform it into a resource.

In fact, one of the most unique and powerful parts of the Generative Coaching process is our attitude towards obstacles. Rather than trying to avoid obstacles, break them down and clear them away, we're actually embracing them as a key part of the creative process. Without obstacles, without conflicting perspectives, there is no true creativity. We also consider addressing obstacles to be a key part of the ecology of the change process.

So it really benefits us to look deeply into the question of *"what is the core, what is the nature of these negative experiences and why are they happening at this moment?"* And the basic idea of Generative Coaching is that these seemingly negative experiences at their core represent the competencies or the resources needed in order to move forward.

That core of these experiences is actually neither good nor bad. It is an energy or a competency. And what determines how it gets expressed is the state of our filters – whether they are in a COACH state or a CRASH state (neuromuscular lock). Our approach to dealing with obstacles is creative non-violence; emphasizing the importance of their transformation and integration as a necessary part of Generative

Change. So, one of our fundamental goals at step five is to identify **CRASH states** (problems/obstacles) and creatively transform them back into **COACH states** (positive resources).

And so we really emphasize this two-level theory of reality construction. At the primary level, things are organized like quantum packets, deep structures or archetypes that can be experienced and expressed in an infinite number of different ways. They represent universal needs and universal resources.

Obstacles as Generative Complementarities

In Generative Coaching, we essentially view obstacles as an attempt to bring balance and wholeness into the system. That's our fundamentally positive understanding of why and when negative experiences consistently arise in the course of a creative path. The reason obstacles show up in a negative form is because an attempt to bring balance has become distorted by a CRASH state.

The great Swiss psychologist Carl Jung said, *"The unconscious is always compensating for the biases of the conscious."* For example, if my conscious mind thinks something like, *"I am too fat, I need to lose weight,"* and I put myself on a strict diet, what do you think I am going to start dreaming about after a week? Celery? Chopped salad? No. More likely something like chocolate cake and ice cream.

We like to say that the basic psychological unit is a relationship of opposites. Carl Jung resurrected the ancient Greek term *"enantiodromia"* to describe this dynamic. *Enantio* means *"containing its opposite."* *Dromos* means to *"run its course."* So "enantiodromia" means that **everything eventually becomes its opposite**; i.e., turns into its opposite. As the ancient Greek philosopher Heraclitus wrote *"cold things become warm, warm things cool, wet things dry and parched things get wet."* So, breathing out becomes breathing in, becomes breathing out, and so on.

So, for every part of a system that says, *"I want to do this,"* there's another part of the system that needs to do the opposite in order to offset or balance it. And we need to be able to positively welcome both sides, *"There's a part of me that really wants to be open with you, and there's a part of me that really needs to stay closed and safe within myself."* We need to feel those as part of the same rhythm – I need to say *"Yes"* and I need to say *"No."* I need to put myself out, I need to bring myself in. I need to work hard, I need to rest. I need to give to other people, I need to receive something for me.

One of us had a client who said, *"For the next year of my life, my intention is to live a freewheeling existence. I want to just be openly spontaneous to everything and have no plans and no rules."* As a generative coach we would humorously start to wonder who is the *"evil twin"* locked in the basement? Who is the complementary self? If I'm going to live my own freewheeling life, what about my sense of duty to everybody else who depends on me?

Which is more important, a sense of commitment to your family or a sense of commitment to your own freewheeling path? Is your family more important than your freewheeling path, or do you think, *"To heck with family. It's every man and woman for themselves."* Clearly, there needs to be some type of balance.

Balancing Generative Complementarities

So, when we state these complements in such obvious terms, we hope it is apparent that these are part of the same creative rhythm. A good representation of this is the Taoist Yin and Yang symbol. Usually when we think of "open and closed," or "light and shadow," we think of one of those as "good" and the other as "bad." So, the light is "good," the shadow is "bad." But in this model, they are not good or bad. In the *I Ching, the Book of Changes*, the characters are the sun turning into moon, turning into sun, turning into moon.

One of the questions we often ask our students and clients is, *"Is it better to breathe in or is it better to breathe out? Which is better?"* The answer is usually something like, *"Well, it kind of depends on which one you have just been doing."* Then we will ask, *"Okay. Is it better to rest or to be full of energy?"* At this point, some people might start saying, *"Well, it's better to be full of energy".* We will then ask, *"Is it better to feel sadness or to feel joy?"* Most people will say, *"It is better to feel joy!"* But really all three are the same question.

Consider, what is more important: to connect with others, or to connect with yourself? For many of our clients, it's one or the other. It's either "my duty to the family" or "my own commitment to take care of myself." And when we assign rigid values like the one side is good and the other is bad, it creates a problem.

As an example, we were doing a seminar in Germany some years ago. There was a woman there who became quite noticeable during the program. Every once in a while we would hear this "bang" because she had gone to sleep and fallen out of her chair onto the ground. We admit that it is not unheard of for people go to sleep at our workshops, but this seemed a bit exaggerated. We asked, "Is it us?" She said, "No, no, it happens all the time." She said that she had been given a diagnosis of "narcolepsy" and could suddenly fall asleep at any time.

So we agreed to do some coaching work with her. But, beforehand, we made a bet with each other about what we would discover regarding her family system. What could her narcolepsy be balancing? What was her family system like? What did we think would be opposite of those narcoleptic symptoms? Did we think that she grew up in a family were people really valued rest and made sure that she got good sleep and took care of herself?

It turned out she came from an immigrant family. They came to the country penniless and without education, and had worked really hard to succeed. Her mother became a doctor and her father was a schoolteacher. Their family motto was: *"a hundred and ten percent effort a hundred percent of the time."* Imagine if you grew up in a family where giving a hundred percent is not good enough. It has to be a hundred and ten percent effort all of the time. What symptom might your unconscious develop to bring balance into that field?

We would all probably agree that "taking a rest" is a universal need. And stored in the unconscious is an ocean of many-many-many possible ways that you can take a rest. And so when you need to take a rest, the universal pattern starts to activate. As it goes through your nervous system, the second level is how you meet and greet it. This quantum potential collapses from infinite possibilities to a specific actuality.

So, we need rest. But when taking a rest goes through the filter *"rest is bad,"* it shows up in a negative form. If we want to transform that into a resource, we say to the symptomatic expression, *"Welcome."* We bring a positive connection, a positive filter and invite the person to discover how to rest in a variety of very interesting positive ways.

Holding Generative Complementarities in a COACH State

Thus, as a deep structure is coming through your set of filters, the state of those filters is going to determine how it becomes expressed as a surface structure. So if my filters are in one state, that deep structure expresses one way. If my filters are in a different state, the exact same deep structure comes out in a different form. If those filters are essentially in a CRASH state, the need to take a rest, for example, can become something like narcolepsy. If the same archetypal need is coming through a COACH state, it will take a more integrated form. It's the same essential deep structure, the same essential archetypal pattern, expressed through a different state of our filters.

When both sides of a balancing set of complementarities are expressed through CRASH filters, it creates an escalating polarization that puts the system even more out of balance. It would be like a client saying, *"I just want to keep breathing out, but I am compelled to breathe in. And the symptom is getting worse! The harder I try to stop it, the stronger the compulsion to breathe in becomes!"*

So we have a slightly more complex diagram to represent that than our big circle and little circle. Inside of a little circle are two other little circles.

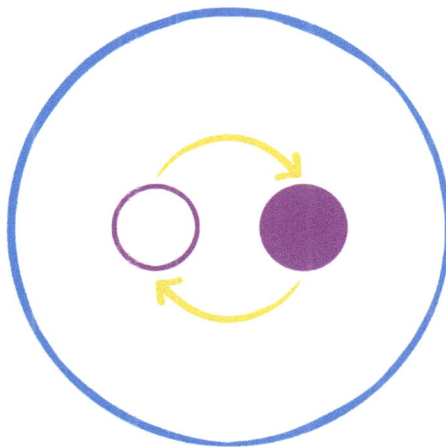

The two little circles represent a pair of generative complementarities. One could be "breathe out" and the other "breathe in," for instance. One could be "go" the other "stop." Or "work" and "rest." If I hold that relationship in the bigger circle of a CRASH state, it's going to continue to become even more and more disconnected, exaggerated and bipolar.

One of us worked with a client, for example, who said, *"You have got to help me relax."* She was asked, *"Out of curiosity, do you drink coffee?"* And she said, *"Yes. 18 cups a day."* The response to that was, *"Sister, you got to back off the caffeine. I can't help you to relax if you drink 18 cups of coffee a day."* She said, *"I can't back off. I have to have that much coffee."* So, the next question was, *"If you didn't drink coffee all day long, what would happen?"* She thought for a while, and responded, *"I would get into bed, I would pull the covers over my head and I would never get up."* So, in her map of the world, those are the two polarized choices; either drink 18 cups of coffee or get into bed and never get up.

This is one of the key challenges we need to recognize in Generative Coaching. The more a client forces one side of a natural complementarity, the more the other side struggles to create balance. This is the reason that Milton Erickson would claim that *"the symptom is the solution."*

Obstacles as Resources

If you meet this attempt to balance the energy and the system with a welcoming presence like in the martial art of Aikido, it has this opportunity to be in relationship and in connection. Then you can explore it's actual intention. When it relaxes, it is capable of shifting and shaping itself in many different ways. When you try to control it or resist it, it has a sense of, *"I feel I'm not allowed here, I'm not welcomed here, I have to fight."* Its only way of thinking is in terms of violence or disconnection. That is not innate or intrinsic in the experience. It is a reflection of the human relationship to the experience.

So, what we bring into this process in Generative Coaching is a mindful, positive, curious, skillful connection. It is a very simple recipe here. It states, if you bring this archetypal energy or pattern through a CRASH state and it is met with a CRASH state, you are going to get a negative expression of it. You are going to get a so-called problem or obstacle. When you can welcome the same archetypal pattern or energy in a generative state, you will get a creative resource.

One of us was coaching a woman whose family worked constantly, and were very successful super achievers. What kind of obstacle do you think she came in with? Chronic fatigue. The family was horrified. She couldn't get out of bed. So, part of the coaching process was to say, *"Let's take a little moment to slow down. We'd like to say to that part of you that is experiencing chronic fatigue, welcome. I'm sure that you're bringing something important into the system. We would like to welcome you into the conversation."* And then she was asked, if that part of her could speak, what its positive intention was? What its need was? And she said, *"I just want to surrender."* Now, is that good or bad? Or is it deeper? One way or another, it's going to get you. You are going to surrender.

And then she paused and she said, *"But I like my work so much."* She developed public health systems for poor communities in a major city. Her programs were incredibly generative. She saved the lives of hundreds of kids. These programs were specialized to support poor families and children.

So, in her map of the world, she either works like a demon or she goes and lays on the beaches of California and quits her job and just relaxes. What do you think you should advise her? Beaches of California or "get back to work and don't be so lazy?" What do you think?

The thing is, there's a thousand miles of unexplored territory in between the two polarities. So, how can you open to the experience of surrender? What does surrender look like? Chronic fatigue or depression or drinking alcohol would be one way, but there are infinite possibilities for experiencing surrender. So, when we say *"welcome,"* that pattern relaxes. And now I can slip back into the ocean of infinite possibilities and say, *"I could surrender by laying in bed, I can go to the beach or I can go to work, or I could surrender moment by moment with each breath and come back home to myself. And discover in each moment what does surrender look like right now."* It allows me to be happy and serve whatever I'm trying to do.

When you can hold that relationship between generative complementarities in a larger COACH field, it is going to become something that looks more like the Yin-Yang symbol.

Welcoming Obstacles

According to the principles of Generative Change, we don't have to try to get rid of big chunks of our experience. We believe that, no matter what we encounter, if we give ourselves a little bit of time and a little bit of connection, we can make creative use of whatever life gives us to become happier and more successful as human beings.

Do you think if you had that as a basic confidence, it would change the way that you operate in the world? Of course, it would. And this is one of the things that Generative Coaching can help people develop a humble confidence about.

To support that, there is a four-part relational "mantra" that we use, which you've have observed us both say many times already in the demonstrations. These are derived from our work and studies with our mutual mentor Milton Erickson.

1. Whenever we meet an obstacle or potential obstacle, the first thing we're going to say is, *"That's interesting."* And we are genuinely curious and interested. "Isn't that amazing? Every time that you go to act on your intention, this obstacle shows up? Isn't that amazing?" This sense of deep curiosity was one of Dr. Erickson's most powerful resources.

2. *"I'm sure it makes sense."* Don't ask me what it is yet, I'm the last one to figure it out. But I know it makes sense. That relates to this idea that everything has some positive purpose. As we have been pointing out in this chapter, obstacles are minimally an attempt to create some type of balance or wholeness. Even if they are coming through some very distorted CRASH form, there is still some positive purpose or intention behind them.

3. *"Something is trying to wake up. Something needs to be held, heard and possibly healed."* That's what all the commotion is about. That's what the disturbance in the field is. Some soul energy is trying to bring a new part of experience to help you grow and evolve. Some key part of your larger holon needs to be acknowledged, understood, resourced and given its place.

4. *"Welcome."* We don't say welcome randomly. We are acknowledging that these presences are part of our larger holon. What appear as obstacles are not inherently negative; they will become negative if you regard them negatively. What makes them negative is the human cursing of them. It's the relationship with them. As Nick LeForce pointed out in the poem at the beginning of this chapter, if your relationship with them is as their enemy, guess what? They are. If your relationship with them is as a resource, guess what? That's what they become.

THAT IS INTERESTING...

I'M SURE IT MAKES SENSE...

*SOMETHING IS TRYING TO WAKE UP.
SOMETHING NEEDS TO BE HELD, HEARD OR HEALED...*

WELCOME

WELCOME

We try to remember before each Generative Coaching session that effectively we are functioning as midwives for our clients. These mantras help us to remind ourselves that this person is coming, no matter what their cover story is, because something inside of them is trying to awaken or be born. Something in their soul is trying to come into the world. So, we want to be able to feel that beneath the story, because the story usually is not directly or accurately naming it. We want to feel what is trying to awaken and then say, *"Welcome."* And then, be able to be a human presence that accompanies the person, so that they can bring all of their being into the world and say, *"My soul belongs to me. I'm an ally, I'm a friend of this all."*

Reconciling Conflicting Opposites

The following steps summarize our basic prototype for the process of transforming obstacles into resources.

1. Develop a **COACH state** (centered, open, alert and connected to resources)

2. Identify **the obstacle** using the statement: *"I want X, but Y stops me."*

3. Tune to "X" **(the intention)**. Sense its center, develop a positive connection (using the relational mantras). Self-scale to an optimal level (7 out of 10 or above).

4. Tune to "Y" **(the obstacle)** Sense its center, develop a positive connection (using the relational mantras). Self-scale to an optimal level (7 out of 10 or above).

5. Move attention between X and Y to **create a resonance** connection between them. Sense how X and Y are complementary aspects of the same resource.

6. Use self-scaling to **ensure a balance** between X and Y, then suggest deepening of the resonance link to promote a generate integration.

7. As integration occurs, **orient to the future intention** and note any positive new responses.

An important part of this process is using self-scaling to make sure that there is a strong enough positive connection to each part – which would be minimally 7 out of 10 or above. This is because if there is a very strong presence and connection to one side (say 9) and a weak connection to the other side (say 3), it will naturally create an imbalance. So we want to be sure to get an approximately equal level of connection to each side. That is what we mean by "optimizing the X and Y intensity levels."

Demonstration of Transforming Conflicting Parts with Somatic Centering

The following is a transcript from a coaching session Steve did in one of our programs in which he guides a client through this basic prototype for reconciling and integrating what appear to be conflicting opposites.

Stephen: *So I want to give you the simple somatic model for this process. It goes "bleep"* (touches his heart with his right hand), *"bleep"* (touches his belly with his left hand), *"whoop, whoop, whoop"* (moves his hands back and forth between the heart and belly).

So we've got two conflicting sides. And we sense where does one live most deeply in the body. "Bleep." (Touches his heart with his right hand.) *We welcome it, create a space for it and begin to move it to a COACH state. Then we've got the other side of the conflicting relationship. Where does that live in the body? "Bleep."* (Touches his belly with his left hand.) *We welcome that, open a place for that and move it to a COACH state as well. So we take the two sides and we define their somatic centers in the body. We create a positive connection to one side and a positive connection to the other side, using the relational mantras. And then we feel what happens when there's a balanced and fluid energetic flow between them. "Whoop. Whoop. Whoop."* (Moves his hands back and forth between the head and belly.) *And only when you feel this balanced flow between the two opposites, you then begin to reorient toward what you are looking to create.*

So let's see how that might happen in our coaching session here. What we're saying is, one of the most sustained formulas is for creating something totally new is to take opposites and hold them simultaneously in the same COACH field. A good way to start is to sense an area in your life where you think, "Well, I would really like to be moving ahead and experiencing this or creating that but I run into some type of obstacle or resistance."

One simple way to find that in a coaching conversation is in terms of a two-part statement. The first part is, "What I want to create is this." And the second part is "But that happens instead, or that stops me." (To client) I am wondering if you have a pair that you think would be interesting to work with here.

Client: *Yes. I have a desire to start a new project and to attribute all my energy to it, but I get distracted and lose focus. Then I don't even know where to look and which first step to make.*

Stephen: *So what would you say that you most passionately want?*

Client: *To make events.*

Stephen: *What would be an example?*

Client: *As a trainer or an organizer.*

Stephen: *Super. And number one on the fantasy list would be …?*

Client: *Where there are a lot of people and they get benefit from it. And they thank me, they thank the speakers, they are happy. I just had one of those. It was really small, but it was very successful.*

Stephen: *That's awesome. If you connect with that, where do you feel it most deeply in your body?*

Client: *Here. (Touches her heart.)*

Stephen: *That's awesome. I'd like to just say to that presence, this passion in your heart, "Welcome. Welcome." It's great. Huh? You feel this deep passion to create these events. And we are doing this process just to say welcome with the hands, with the breath, with the mind.*

Say "Hello." Great. This place in your heart is filled with a passionate interest. That's great. Welcome. Thank you for joining us in this conversation. What happens when you hear me say that?

Client: *It is pleasant. I feel your support.*

Stephen: *On a scale one to ten how much do you feel this connection in your heart?*

Client: *Nine.*

Stephen: *Where does this number come from?*

Client: *I don't know.*

Stephen: *Do you feel it's coming from here?* (Points to her head.) *Or here?* (Points to her heart.)

Client: *From here.* (Touches her heart.)

Stephen: *Awesome. So, there is this positive passion inside of you that wants to create these positive events. Can we just take a few moments just to breath with that? Feel how deeply that lives inside of you. You could see it. You could sense it. Each day you could learn to understand it and support it. Welcome. So you see, we are thinking about this ego mind* (touches his head) *as sort of a manager or a representative. And the creative passion is coming from is a different place* (touches his heart).

Client: *I feel it here.* (Touches her heart.)

Stephen: *Cool. That's good to know. So then in that process, as you go and take that passion and transfer it into reality, what starts to happen? What shuts it down or blocks it?*

Client: *It's kind of lack of focus when I start thinking about how to realize it.*

Stephen: *I cannot help but notice that I see this tension in your shoulders. I am curious where this part that is more tense, where that lives inside of you? When you've got such a big dream, that you really want to create these events, and then something happens where you lose your focus.*

Client: *It lives here.* (Touches her diaphragm.)

Stephen: *Isn't that interesting? As you step up to that threshold, somebody down here* (points to her diaphragm) *says: "Wait a second! Wait for me. I am coming too." I am sure that makes sense. As you go to live your dream, there is some fear or pressure that also awaits to come forward. I would ask you to let a number come that represents an age of that part that gets scared.*

Client: *I have the number five.*

Stephen: *Just for your information. When I ask these questions, I am always asking my own creative mind to answer them from my perspective. What came up for me was four. Isn't that nice? As you go to really make a difference in the world, there is a younger part of you that says: "Hey, wait for me. Wait for me. I want to come" So, I invite you to just close your eyes for a moment and feel the deepest core of this younger fear in that place deep inside. I hope it is okay to say to that place, "Welcome. Welcome." And I am sure that whatever you are bringing is really important to be able to*

make the dream come true. That is why I would say, "Welcome. Welcome. Welcome. Welcome."

Client: *Welcome*

Stephen: *And what happens as you feel that positive welcoming?*

Client: *I feel how I relax.*

Stephen: *I have sort of an interesting question. What might it be like to have a partnership between of these two parts of you that seem to be already deeply connected? What do you think about that idea?*

Client: *I haven't thought about it. That's interesting.*

Stephen: *So, maybe we could do the beginning of a process that I would encourage you to be practicing and exploring. I think we would both agree, that to make that dream come true, it is kind of important to be connecting to all different parts of you. So as you move towards creating those amazing events, you feel the support of that part of you that says, "Yeah, let's do it!"* (points to her heart) *and the part that says, "Oh, my...oh no"* (points to her diaphragm). *And to feel that they are all part of the same creative family. So, let me just invite you, if you feel comfortable, to say "I really want to create these big events and to do that I feel my connection here"* (gestures to heart) *and bring that energy into play. "And then I feel my connection here"* (gestures to diaphragm) *and bring that energy into play. And feel what happens, when you just move your attention to the connection back and forth between the two as you make the statement "I want to create this big event."*

Client: *I want to create events, feeling the connection in here* (touches her heart), *and sensing this force, feeling this connection here* (touches her diaphragm).

Stephen: *And experience that all the way through your whole body. What happens when these parts just go through all of you?* (To audience) *I don't know if you could see, she started that movement as a young girl. And then I saw this powerful young woman, ready to emerge.* (To client) *Shall we do it again?*

So, "as I am going to create these events with passion (points to her heart) *. . . Welcome. Welcome. Welcome."* *And then the Yin energy, gentle, powerful, vulnerable* (points to diaphragm). *Relax the shoulders, bring it throughout your whole body. And let it create the connection between the two of them.* (Points back and forth between her heart and her diaphragm.) *And feel that power. How is that?*

Client: *Great. Pleasant. I feel lighter in the body.*

Stephen: *This last piece is just touching on something that you could practice on your own. It is to set the intention "I really want to create these big events" and then just notice how it activates the one side. Each time you say "I have got the passion to do something big," you can go to that place, where your mind connects with that deeper source. And any time when you feel the pressure, the fear, you can say "Oh, my vulnerable power just showed up. That's interesting, and then feel the whole of me."* (Sings) *"Why not to take all of me?" You do not need to sing this song.* (Laughs.) *But a little bit of this and a little bit of that. How old are you?*

Client: *Twenty six.*

Stephen: *That's awesome. What I sense in you reminds me of what Robert and I were doing at 26. It is really nice to see the next generation coming into this field. We are the old timers. I sincerely send you lots and lots of support for bringing both your passion and your vulnerability together.*

Client: *Thank you very much.*

Stephen: *Is it okay if we stop here?*

Client: *Yes.*

Stephen: *Is there anything you want to share with the group about your experience?*

Client: *I have an interesting observation that you do not need to transform this fear and this feeling of confusion, but you can just accept it and come between them and find the interaction of these parts.*

Stephen: *Fantastic. You stated that more succinctly than either of us could say. It takes us three days to say what you just said in one sentence.*

Transforming conflicting parts with somatic centering

ACKNOWLEDGING "WHAT I WANT" AND "WHAT GETS IN THE WAY", AND WHERE YOU FEEL THEM IN THE BODY

WELCOME

WELCOMING AND LISTENING TO THE MESSAGE OF EVERY PART THAT NEEDS ATTENTION

MOVING YOUR ATTENTION FROM ONE CENTER TO THE OTHER ONE TO INTEGRATE THEM

PRACTICE RECONNECTING WITH BOTH CENTERS AND PROJECTING YOUR INTENTION INTO THE FUTURE

Using Somatic Models to Work with Obstacles

In working with obstacles as part of a pair of generative complementarities, we find that using somatic models can be very helpful to clarify and shift the conflictual nature of the relationship. As example, one of us had a client who expressed his intention as, *"I want to finish writing this book! I'm past the deadline! I have to finish writing it!"* The response to this was, *"Okay, that's great! Go do it!"* To which he said, *"But I always end up procrastinating. I need your help to stop doing that."* So in that type of languaging you can see that procrastination sounds really negative. And often the request is to *"assassinate the obstacle."* *"I'm going to pay you lot of money! I just want you to kill the symptom. No questions asked. Nothing personal. Just business."*

As a generative coach, however, we view the perception of the perceived obstacle as something "negative" to actually be the primary issue. We want to help the client to consider, "How is it that every time I go to finish the book, I end up procrastinating? What is the relationship between those to sides?" And the basic idea in Generative Change is that the procrastination, or the symptom, or the problem, represents the other side of the whole solution pattern.

So, in this example with *"finish the book – procrastination,"* how do you open a conversational space, in which both of these sides can be brought into a more generative and productive relationship? A powerful way to do that is to represent the two sides as somatic models. In this instance, the client was asked to take the intention *"I want to finish the book"* and to *"show that as a somatic model."* In response the client resolutely set his jaw, furrowed his brow and clenched both of his fists.

So, how long do you think he'll last in this state? Do you think he'll be able to achieve his intention in this state? What do you think will happen after a maximum of ten minutes? What do you think is going to follow it? When he was asked, *"So, now show me the somatic model for what you're calling procrastination,"* his response was to drop his head, shoulders and arms as if he were falling down.

"I WANT TO FINISH WRITING THIS BOOK!"

"BUT I ALWAYS END UP PROCRASTINATING"

GETTING INTO A COACH STATE

Now what do you notice about both of the somatic models? Which one is **COACH** and which one is **CRASH**? They are actually two different forms of CRASH. That's the real problem.

So, to use somatic modeling, we would translate the verbal talk about the situation into simple somatic representations. In this example, we say, *"Show me your somatic representation of the part of you that really has this commitment to finishing the book."* (Sets jaw, furrows brow and clenches both fists.) *"Great. Welcome. Welcome."* *"Now, show me the part that procrastinates."* (Drops head, shoulders and arms as if falling down.) *"Oh, I see. That's amazing! Welcome! Isn't that incredible?"*

So now we want to translate them into their **COACH** version. We say, *"So let's get a COACH state. Great. And only in a way that you stay centered and connected, step into that somatic model of your intention."* Now I'm looking for any places of CRASH. I might say, *"Relax your eyeballs. And feel that like a tai chi movement. You really want to finish the book."* (Jaw releases, eyebrows are more relaxed and fists are more loose and moving back and forth.) *"That's great."*

"And then, only in a way that you can stay in a COACH state, invite that part that you've called previously procrastination." (Opens arms, brings hands to the side and breathes deeply.) *"That's great. That's great. So would you call this a problem, do you think? What's the difference?"*

"And now, find the state in which you can feel both at the same time as a whole pattern. Every time I start writing, I feel this need to relax. Commitment. (Focuses eyes and brings hands in front of body.) *Relaxation.* (Opens arms, brings hands to the side and breathes deeply.). *Commitment.* (Focuses eyes and brings hands in front of body.) *Relaxation.* (Opens arms, brings hands to the side and breathes deeply.) That's great. *"And so now you see they are not mutually exclusive, they are complementary. Just like breathing out and breathing in."*

And this guy, by the way, published three books in the two years since that session. So we see that that obstacle was really what his creative consciousness was bringing to make his performance state whole.

SOMATIC MODEL OF "FINISHING THE BOOK" IN COACH STATE

SOMATIC MODEL OF "PROCRASTINATING" IN COACH STATE

GOING FROM ONE TO THE OTHER TO FEEL BOTH AT THE SAME TIME

Somatic Modeling of Conflicting Parts

The following are the basic steps of our prototype for applying somatic modeling to transform conflicting parts back into generative complementarities.

1. Establish a **COACH (generative) state.**

2. **Identify the conflict** using the statement: *"I want to do X, but Y interferes."*

3. Create a **somatic model** (physical gesture and movement) of the intention (X).

4. Create a **somatic model** (physical gesture and movement) representing the obstacle (Y).

5. **Welcome each part** and bring awareness to where in the body any CRASH shows up.

6. Find the COACH expression of the **somatic model of the intention** (X). Identify its positive intention.

7. Find the COACH expression of the **somatic model of the obstacle** (Y). Identify its positive intention.

8. Staying in a COACH state, and keeping in mind the positive intentions of the two parts, **practice moving back and forth** between the somatic model of the obstacle to the somatic model of the intention slowly, mindfully and rhythmically. What new possibilities emerge?

9. As integration occurs, **orient to the future intention** and note any positive new responses.

The following is a transcript from a coaching session Robert did in one of our programs in which he guides a client through this process. The transcript picks up after Robert has established a COACH state together with the client.

Robert: *So, I am curious to know what is it that you really want to create in your life?*

Client: *I want to fulfill a project and I even have a team, that is an international team, and also I have an investor already. And they all gathered together to manifest my vision.*

Robert: *Wow. That's fantastic!*

Client: *I have all of this gathered around me, but I don't feel worth it.*

Robert: *That's interesting. Let's pause for just a moment. I hear you saying that you have a vision for a project and, in fact, you already have a whole group of people that is coming to you to support you in that vision. And yet at the same time you feel that "I am not worth it."*

Client: *Yes. That's right.*

Robert: *So we want to make space to welcome all of that. And I would like to first bring a little more attention to your intention. Because, it is interesting, right now I know the situation but actually don't know what your intention is. What is it that you most passionately want?*

Client: *What I really want is to feel strong and worthy to create.*

Robert: *Let's pause and really connect with that intention, "I really want to feel myself strong and worthy to create." Breathe that through your body so that you can feel the resonance. "I am strong and I am worthy to create. I really do want to feel that."*

Client: (Takes a deep breath and places hands just below her diaphragm.)

Robert: *I am curious. I saw you were already putting your hands there* (gestures to diaphragm) *several times. Is that where you most feel that?*

Client: *I feel some kind of support for my intention here in my center.* (Takes a deep breath and places hands just below her diaphragm.)

Robert: *Okay, great. I feel support for my intention here.* (Mirrors her gesture.) *So now, we want to turn those words into a somatic model. If you were going to show with your body what it is like to be strong and worthy to create, how would you do it? If you couldn't tell that to me, but you had to show me what you wanted with a gesture and movement, how would you show it?*

Client: (Extends her arms out from her diaphragm, raises them over her head and pumps both fists in front of her.)

Robert: (Mirrors the gesture.) *Nice. And I just want to say, "Welcome. I see your strength. I see your worthiness to create. Welcome. It is good to be strong." I am curious, when you make that gesture, how strongly do you feel the presence of this intention, zero to ten?*

Client: *Ten.*

Robert: *Ten! I like that. Let's do that again. What I really want is this…* (Both extend their arms out from the diaphragm, raise them over their heads and pump both fists in front of them.) *Welcome. And, of course, we know that there is a "but" here. I want to do this, but...*

Client: *I am not worth it.* (Drops her head and shoulders and leans over with her hands on her abdomen.)

Robert: *Oh, that came quickly.*

Client: *Yes. I have a good connection with that.*

Robert: *That's great! Seriously, that's great!*

Client: *That is ten, too.*

Robert: *So, "I really want to feel myself strong and worthy to create (*extends arms out from the diaphragm, raises them over his head and pumps both fists) *but this happens instead."* (Drops his head and shoulders and leans over with his hands on his abdomen.) *"Welcome." I am absolutely sure that makes perfect sense. I am sure that it is not random. I am sure this is here for a very good reason. In fact, as you do that, it is an interesting question to ask, what age would this feeling of "I am not worth it" be? If you just let a number come.*

Client: (Drops her head and shoulders and leans over with her hands on her abdomen.) *Two or three.*

Robert: *I just want to welcome that two or three year-old presence. I am sure that she is a big package of life force. I really want to welcome her. I am just curious, we can see that there's a lot of CRASH in that somatic model of her. But actually you said you have good connection there. And staying connected beneath the CRASH, let's bring awareness to this part of you. Make the same movement, really being aware of what's going on.*

Client: (Lowers her head and shoulders slowly and carefully brings her hands to her abdomen.)

Robert: *What is this 2 or 3 year-old saying? Something needs to be heard or healed. What does she need? What is her intention?*

Client: *To feel love and care.*

Robert: *That's interesting. I noticed something interesting; that this gesture has spontaneously shifted a little bit. Instead of that* (drops his head and shoulders and leans over with his hands on his abdomen) *it became like this* (lowers his head and shoulders slowly and carefully brings his hands to his abdomen). *And, I think it could be really interesting to just come from this* (lowers his head and shoulders slowly and carefully brings his hands to his abdomen) *to that* (extends arms out from the diaphragm, raises them over his head and pumps both fists). *And instead of stopping, come back to this* (lowers his head and shoulders slowly and carefully brings his hands to his abdomen) *and then that* (extends arms out from the diaphragm, raises them over his head and pumps both fists). *Exploring all the space in between this* (lowers his head and shoulders slowly and carefully brings his hands to his abdomen) *and that* (extends arms out from the diaphragm, raises them over his head and pumps both fists).

Client: (Slowly moves back and forth between the two gestures.)

Robert: *I am really curious, if you can really feel the presence of all of you. We welcome first what you really want to do, "strength, worthy to create."* (Extends arms out from the diaphragm, raises them over his head and pumps both fists.) *Welcome. And then feel that other connection to the intention "to feel love and care."* (Lowers his head and shoulders slowly and carefully brings his hands to his abdomen.) *Welcome.*

Client: (Continues to slowly move back and forth between the two gestures.)

Robert: *That's interesting. That's right. Wanting to feel strong and worthy. Wanting to feel love and care. Beautiful. That's right.*

Client: (Begins to make a rhythmic movement, like a dance, gesturing out from her body and bringing her arms and hands back to her body and then extending out again.)

Robert: (Mirrors the movement.) *Ah. That's interesting. Something new. I am curious what happened when you were doing that?*

Client: (Smiles broadly.) *I don't know.*

Robert: *"I don't know." I love the way your smile comes when you do that. What do you notice that is happening? You don't have to understand it, but is there any new sensation?*

Client: *I felt being separate before into two parts. This little weak one and this strong one. But the weak one always won.*

Robert: *That is interesting. That it's those weak vulnerable parts that always seem to win. I know that Stephen would agree with me about this, those seemingly vulnerable parts are actually where our greatest creativity comes from – especially when they feel loved and cared for. That three-year old is the one that has the creativity and then I can bring her creative ideas to my strength and sense of worth. Good to know.*

Client: (Smiles broadly.) *Yes.*

Robert: *Just out of curiosity, what happens if you think the thought right now "I am not worth it"?*

Client: *It's strange. It no longer seems to fit.*

Robert: *That is an interesting thing to notice. These thoughts that used to torture me now kind of make me go "huh?" because there is no place for them to resonate. Interesting to notice. So now let's just take a moment and walk up the timeline through your storyboard. "Where can I now take my intention, my team, my project?"*

Client: (Walks up her timeline gesturing out from her body and bringing her arms and hands back to her body and then extending out again. After walking a few steps she twirls and makes a triumphant gesture.)

Robert: *That's right. Oh, that's nice. Seems like actually here something went kind of "Whooh!" What happens here?*

Client: *Here I felt for the first time in my body like this project has already been accomplished.*

Robert: *That's interesting. It's good to know. "For the first time I can feel in my body that the project is accomplished." Let's breathe that through. "Yes I can. I can do it." I just want to say, I send you my full support. You can do it!*

Client: *Thank you.*

Robert: *Before we go, is there anything that you would want to share that was either particularly important about what we did, or what happened, that you think was a useful insight? What is it that you will take with you?*

Client: *I will always remember the moment when it didn't resonate anymore that I am not worthy. It was a clear moment, a very clear distinction. And I will bring in my body the feeling that "I can!" Thank you!*

(Applause.)

Working with somatic models to transform and integrate obstacles and conflicts makes Jung's principle of *enantiodromia* very clear and real. One gesture goes into the other, which goes back to the first gesture, which goes into the second one, and so on. The Yang is complemented by the Yin, complemented by the Yang, complemented by the Yin. And then you will notice a little bit of Yin that goes into the Yang and a little bit of Yang starts going into the Yin. So, that is what we would call a generative integration. It becomes continuous unbroken attention, analogue versus digital, one continuous rhythmic movement.

And instead of one OR the other response, you now have a whole spectrum of new possibilities in between. There are many possible combinations and variations of the two complements that might be appropriate or necessary for the wide range of situations in which we may find ourselves.

The next big question is, *"How do I sustain these learnings and changes through time?"* We like to point out that, at the end of a coaching session, nothing has really changed yet. We've opened the possibility for something to change. But in order for the potential to fully manifest, we need to *"get it in the muscle."* That is what our next step of Generative Coaching is about – practices for deepening the change.

Somatic Modeling of Conflicting Parts

FIND A SOMATIC MODEL FOR THE PART THAT EXPRESSES "WHAT I WANT" AT A GOOD LEVEL OF CONNECTION

ACKNOWLEDGING "WHAT I WANT" AND "WHAT GETS IN THE WAY", AND WHERE YOU FEEL THEM IN THE BODY

FIND A SOMATIC MODEL FOR THE PART THAT NEEDS "LOVE AND CARE"

EXPLORE GOING SLOWLY BACK AND FORTH FROM ONE SOMATIC MODEL TO THE OTHER UNTIL IT BECOMES LIKE "A DANCE" OR A "TAI-CHI" MOVEMENT, NOTICING ANY INSIGHTS FROM THIS INTEGRATION

ANTONIO MEZA

Pause Now

Pause now
long enough
to turn
your attention
to the quiet underneath
the noise of the world;
to listen again
to the whispered secrets of your soul,
to return
to what lives at your core
and to embrace, once again,
the unspoken
and unbroken vows of the heart.

Pause now
long enough
to drop the effort
to patch up
the torn and tattered edges of your own life,
to let
what is incomplete in you be
not your prison walls but your gateway
to all
that is yet to come.

Pause now
long enough
to let your breath
be waves of the infinite flowing in and out
until you arrive,
at last,
at the place
where all questions end
and you yourself become endless . . .

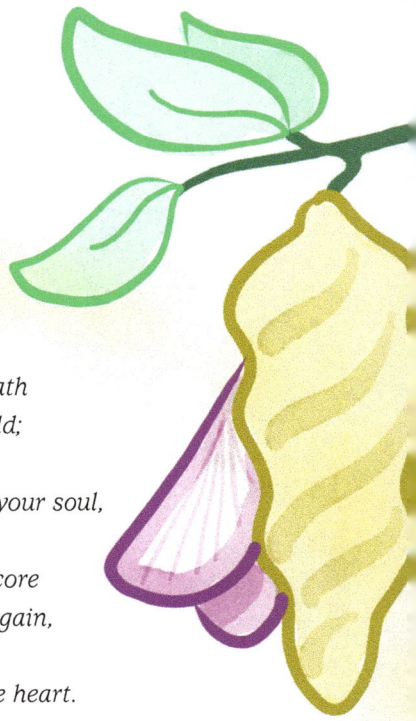

– Nick LeForce

Chapter 8

Step 6
Practices for Deepening and
Sustaining the Change

Step six of the Generative Coaching process is to establish key practices in order to both sustain and deepen the changes that you have begun in the previous five steps. Effective coaching is ultimately grounded in practices. All good sports coaches know that, in order for their team to be successful, players need to spend at least three times as much time practicing as they do actually playing the game. Practice is how you get a new competence "in the muscle." We like to point out that *"you are only as good as your practices."* We could even go so far as to say, *"You are what you practice."*

As we have mentioned previously, what a client has been able to achieve in a particular coaching session really hasn't changed anything yet. It's opened a place of possibility. It's given the client a sense of what's possible and how to be able to make it actual. But in order for that potential to become an ongoing and concrete part of the client's everyday experience, they have to practice. In fact, practice is so important that, when we work with clients, we ask them to make a commitment to at least 30 minutes of practice every day.

The key questions to consider in order to create an effective practice are, "How does the client take what they have learned and developed in the first five steps and keep moving it forward and sustaining it in his or her life? What are going to be the practices that make the changes the client has started become the new baseline for his or her ongoing activity? What are the things that the client is going to be doing again and again to ensure that he or she is ready to effectively express his or her intention in whatever situation arises?"

One form of practice is specific homework related to the intention that the client has been focusing on during the session. We prefer that these are collaboratively generated. We will ask, *"What do you need to do from here in order to keep moving forward? What kind of commitment are you willing to make?"* Frequently, such homework will be a continuation or repetition of one of the processes we went through with the client during the coaching session. It is through homework of this type that clients learn to become their own self-coach. They are remembering the steps of the process and guiding themselves through them. For instance, we may invite them to take some time each morning to access their three positive connections and walk up their timeline through their storyboard to preview their day. This is what we would call a *"preparation"* practice.

Practices can serve several different purposes with respect to supporting an intention. *Preparation* practices help the client to be ready to express their intention in new situations. *Reflection* practices help clients deepen their change by increasing their awareness and understanding of the significant factors that support reaching their intention. *Sustaining* practices strengthen the changes that accompany the intention and help to install the intention as a new baseline.

Preparation Practices

Effective preparation helps us to ensure that we are in the best state from which to effectively express our intention in whatever situation arises. Starting each significant activity of the day in COACH state would be an example of a preparation practice. When we hold team meetings, for instance, we always take a few moments to be sure we are all in a COACH state and connected with one another and then set our intention for the meeting.

Some common types of preparation practices include mental rehearsal, motivation and anchoring.

Mental Rehearsal

A basic prototype for mental rehearsal as a preparation practice would involve:

1. Enter a **COACH state** and connect to your intention (verbally, visually and somatically).
2. **Identify the situation** (from your storyboard) in which you want to express your intention.
3. **Picture what you would like to do** in your mind's eye, as if you are an observer watching it on a video. (If it is difficult to imagine what you would do, you can think of a role model and picture what they would do.)
4. **Put yourself into your mental picture** and into the situation, and imagine you are doing and experiencing what you pictured. See, hear and feel the scenario as if you are actually living it.
5. **Create a somatic model** for the successful expression of your intention in that situation.

Increasing Motivation

It can be important to include motivation in a preparation practice as well. The following is a core prototype for increasing motivation for a particular intention.

1. **Enter a COACH state** and connect to your intention (verbally, visually and somatically).

2. **Identify the situation** (from your storyboard) in which you want to express your intention.

3. Stepping into that situation on your timeline, **imagine that you have already achieved your intention** in that situation, and are really enjoying it. Get in touch with what you are seeing, hearing, doing and feeling while enjoying these benefits. Create a **somatic model** for that feeling of success.

4. **Enhance or adjust any sensory qualities of the experience** in such a way that it feels more motivating or compelling. Does the experience become more compelling and attractive if you add more color? Brightness? Sound? Words? Movement? Identify which qualities make the experience feel the best. Applying those qualities, experience the good feelings that come from achieving your intention.

5. **Remember those feelings** as you picture yourself doing the things that you know will help you move closer to your intention. (You can create a self-anchor in order to help transfer those feelings.)

Generative Coaching

Self-Anchoring

Building and strengthening the inner resources necessary to reach our intentions is another important practice. This can be supported and reinforced through the process of self-anchoring. This involves creating an associative connection between the resource experience and a trigger that we can bring with us into the situation in which we want to express our intention. The basic prototype for creating a self-anchor for a resource is:

1. **Remember a time** when you experienced the resourceful state strongly. See what you saw, hear what you heard and feel what you felt as vividly as you can.

2. **Find something to use as an anchor** to ground and trigger your resource state. (An object, mental picture, key word, gesture, etc.)

3. Put yourself back into the resourceful experience. See what you saw, hear what you heard and feel what you felt as vividly as you can. **Connect the memory of this experience to your anchor** by shifting your attention momentarily to the cue or trigger and back again to the resourceful experience.

4. Clear your mind and **change your state for a moment**. Do something to distract yourself.

5. **Put your attention on your anchor.** You should immediately get the resourceful feeling. If you don't, repeat steps 3 and 4 a few more times.

Reflection Practices

The purpose of reflection practices is to help clients deepen their change by increasing their awareness and understanding of the significant factors that support reaching their intention. The simplest form of this type of practice is to reflect on significant activities and ask, *"What did I learn from that?"* If everything went well, what did I learn from that? If things did not go well, what did I learn from that?

Scott Miller, who is considered one of gurus of therapy outcome research, has found that the single most important thing that a coach can do to produce the biggest improvement in their coaching sessions is to have their client fill out a simple written feedback form at the end of each session. And even if the coach doesn't read it, simply having the client consider, *"What was helpful for me was . . ."* *"What really worked was . . ."* etc., creates a significant improvement. And if the therapist or coach actually reads t, you get another significant boost.

Having the client keep a journal and bring it in for the next session would be a form of a reflection practice. There is actually a website called "coach.me" that provides a simple tracking methodology for people to measure the frequency of particular behaviors. A person can download an App onto their smartphone and click a button every time they engage in a particular behavior; having a cigarette for example. If somebody wants to track their exercise habits, for instance, every time they exercise, they click on the tracking button. This type of feedback helps to bring greater awareness to the client for what they are doing and what is working.

As another example of homework assignments that can be used for reflection, Milton Erickson would have his clients do metaphorical activities, such as climb Squaw Peak (a mountain near his office in Phoenix, Arizona) or go to the city's Botanical Gardens. He would assign them to come back and report on what they observed and felt. This would function as a type of Rorschach test that would give him information about his client's current state and level of progress.

The Choice Generator

The choice generator is a reflection practice whose purpose is to generate an increasing amount of learning and choice from every experience or life situation. The process involves reviewing the events of the day and identifying the significant choice points relating to the achievement of a particular intention. For each choice point, you are to reflect on the choices you made at those points and whether they were successful or unsuccessful with respect to reaching your intention. Then, you imagine three alternative ways you could have responded, other than the way that you did (whether or not what you did was successful). You then mentally project the results and consequences of each alternative and explore what it would be like to have actually made this choice by stepping into the experience and fully living it somatically in your imagination.

The object of this exercise is not to find the "best way" or "correct way" to respond to a particular situation. Rather it is to get into the habit of creating more and more possibilities. Doing this exercise regularly creates the possibility of getting three times as much experience per day as you would have by simply remembering or recording what actually happened. This type of exercise can significantly accelerate people's ability to learn from their experience.

The following is an outline of the basic steps of the choice generator practice:

1. **Enter into a COACH state** and connect with your intention.

2. **Identify an important experience that happened during the day** in relation to your intention and identify several significant choice points.

3. **Reflect on the choices you made** at those points and whether they were successful or unsuccessful in helping you reach your intention.

4. Stay in your COACH state and open to a resource from your larger field of resources that could support you in that situation. Keeping connected to that resource, put yourself back into the situation and **let an alternative response emerge spontaneously.** Explore what it would be like to have actually made this choice by fully living it somatically in your imagination.

5. **Repeat this process** to create at least three alternative choices for each choice point.

It can also be useful to combine preparation practices with reflection practices. When we are doing workshops together, for instance, we meet for breakfast every morning to prepare the day. After dinner each evening we meet to reflect on what happened during the day and to anticipate the coming day.

Sustaining Practices

The purpose of a sustaining practice is to strengthen and support the achievement of a particular intention through time. To be effective, the purpose and benefits of any practice will need to outweigh any inconvenience it creates. So these are what can be called "high leverage practices." This type of practice involves spending a relatively short period of time each day that delivers a disproportionate cumulative benefit. Think of something like brushing your teeth. If you brush your teeth a few minutes a day, you keep them 20 years longer.

How many of you brush your teeth at least once a day? Why do you do that? In order to keep a certain state of oral health. Similarly, our emotional and psychological health takes daily practice. And, again, you are only as good as your practices.

Of course, many people will say something like, "That sounds like a great idea but can't you see I'm a really busy person, an important person? When I get time, I'll do those the practices, I promise." And twenty years later they are still saying the same thing and wondering why nothing has changed.

People frequently ask us, "You both are so busy, how do you find the time to write all the books that you have written?" The truth is, you will never *find* the time. You have to *make* the time. You are never *given* time for practices, it must be taken. When we are working on a book, like this one for example, we will commit to spend at least half an hour to an hour every morning writing no matter where we are in the world. And that means, even if we have to get up half an hour earlier, that is what we are going to do. A practice is a result of a commitment to making something happen.

If you take a look at our workshop schedules you'll see we are busy beavers. But each of us does at least an hour and a half of practices a day. Robert runs at least 60-90 minutes every day (rain or shine) and Steve meditates and walks. During these periods, we are also frequently incorporating some preparation and reflection practices related to our intentions for the day. We find that if we don't do those practices, we get cranky, we procrastinate, and we start getting into bad habits. We guarantee people, "If you do certain practices you will have more time in your day." You'll start to realize that time is, in a big way, a psychological experience. Secondly you will enjoy your work more and you will do better work.

Virgin Group founder Richard Branson says, "If I run half an hour in the morning I get twice as much done during the day." That is a good example of what we are calling a "high leverage" practice. That half-hour investment doubles your productivity the rest of the day. Conversely, if you say, "Oh gosh I cannot afford that time," you will only get half as much done the remainder of the day. Which is the greater loss of time?

The most important sustaining practices are those that we do for our own self-care. This means not for your work and not for your family or loved ones. Just for you. And if you don't do things to care for yourself, your unconscious will find other ways to do it. In fact, it frequently shows up in the form of a negative habit, addiction or some other type of symptom like the examples from the previous chapter: procrastination, chronic fatigue, narcolepsy, etc.

We could view bad habits and addictions as a form of "practice" in which a person's unconscious is attempting to bring balance or wholeness to their lives in a distorted way. As an example, one of us was coaching a person who wanted to quit smoking. He had smoked for 40 years. Now this man had incredible willpower for practically everything else in his life. He was the kind of person that could stand in the face of a gale-force wind. But he couldn't stop smoking. When we actually welcomed the behavior, it turned out that smoking was the one thing in his life that this man did just for himself. Other smokers have told us that the positive intention of the behavior was to remind them to breathe. That's interesting; paradoxical but interesting. A big part of transforming the smoking addiction for this client was giving himself permission to do other more healthy things in a consistent way "just for himself."

So our self-care is fundamentally important. If you've ever traveled by airplane you have probably heard the announcement, "In case of an emergency, oxygen masks will drop down in front of you. Please pull the mask down toward your face and place the mask over your mouth and nose. If you are traveling with a small child, please put on your mask first, then attend to the child." At first, this advice seems backward. A child in the midst of an emergency would be vulnerable, scared and disoriented and would need attention. But attending to the child's needs first could be disastrous. Why? Because if the adult becomes disoriented or loses consciousness, the child is left to fend for themselves. The adult must be alert, breathing, thinking, and resourceful in order to properly care for the child through the duration of an emergency. If we are incapacitated, we can't be of service or value to anybody else.

This is one of those fundamental complementarities. We need practices to care for ourselves and keep us alert, breathing, thinking, and resourceful so that we can more effectively care for others.

"Météo" – An Example of a Sustaining Practice

Robert and his wife Deborah have a daily practice, based on this principle, that they do when they are in the same place, that they call "météo" (the French word for "weather report"). The purpose of this practice is to tend to their relationship and at the same time tend to themselves and each other. It is not a coaching or problem solving session. It is a sharing, listening and acknowledgment practice.

They alternate responsibility for the practice odd and even days, so one of them is in charge each day for asking the other what time would work well for them. They usually take the time just before dinner. The person responsible for that day (A) guides the process:

1. (A) guides both (A) and (B) to enter a COACH state using some kind of movement to transition into an embodied, present state and release tension from the day

2. As (A) and (B) sit or stand facing one another, (A) guides both (A) and (B) to bring attention present and inward, sensing the state of the internal "weather," listening to what wants to emerge to be shared in this space they are creating together; i.e., the "field" or the container of their relationship

3. (A) asks (B) what (B) would like to share about what is happening for them that day. It's not, "Tell me about the content of your day." Rather, it is, "How are you in there?" Events may come up as part of the sharing, but that is not the focus. The emphasis is on, "How are you feeling in there?"

4. (B) shares (usually a few minutes). It may include experiences of gratitude, concern, joy, anticipation, relief, etc.

5. (A) mirrors back what they hear as accurately as possible (not interpreting or commenting), and it's not a memory test. (B) can help if (A) forgets something.

6. (A) then shares what touches them about what they have heard. It is not a conversation: (B) receives and says thank you.

They then switch and repeat the process with (B) asking (A) what (A) would like to share about his or her day.

The process usually takes about a half an hour. If they are pressed for time, they can do it much more quickly by shortening the beginning processes and just sharing one or two things each.

The point is to share the feeling state, the inner climate, not the content of what they did that day, unless a teeny bit of that is necessary to share about the inner climate. They are also very careful not to use this as a time to air grievances. There is another process for that! This is a safe space to tune in and check in with themselves and one another, and to give each other their full attention.

We contend that practices such as this are extremely important for a balanced and healthy life. These types of sustaining practices should be pleasurable while also quieting the mind, deepening mind-body harmony, and opening to creative consciousness.

Demonstration of Helping a Client Establish a Practice

The following is a transcript of how we might work with a client to collaboratively create a practice. In this case the client, whose professional calling involved her supporting many other people, had the intention of "taking more time for myself." She had identified a resource for this intention as her grandfather (who had died a number of years earlier), who could balance "seriousness with humor."

Coach: *What would be something you could do on a regular basis that would be a really good example of you putting more of this balance into practice, to take more time for yourself?*

Client: *What I would like to do is, in the morning, to walk without my dogs.*

Coach: *Without your dogs.*

Client: *Because I do that, but with the dogs, and it's not the same.*

Coach: *I completely understand, and you're doing it for the dogs rather than for you.*

Client: *Yes, and I have to stop every 3 seconds, with my male dog. (Laughter.)*

Coach: *I know what you're talking about. So, wouldn't that be wonderful? "I'm going to make this commitment to take this time in the morning for a walk just for me. And is there a place where you like to walk?*

Client: *I live in a suburb, so it's green and we have a little river there, so it's very nice.*

Coach: *So, let's imagine, if you were to put yourself there, taking that walk by yourself. See what you see, hear what you hear, feel what you feel.*

Client: *I feel a good feeling of fulfillment. I wanted to do something and I did it.*

Coach: *How often would you need to do this in order to create that balance where you know that you are taking the time for yourself that you need?*

Client: *I think I should do it every day for a while to get a habit.*

Coach: *So, for at least a certain period, you do it every day.*

Client: *Yes.*

Coach: *How long of a period would you need to do that every day, just to make sure it becomes a habit? Would it be two weeks, two months?*

Client: *At least 3 weeks.*

Coach: *At least 3 weeks. Good to know.*

Client: *Because if I do it less, then I'll forget it.*

Coach: *That makes sense. So, are you ready to make the commitment to take a half hour walk by yourself every morning for the next three weeks?*

Client: *I would like to but I am afraid that I'm going to start trading off. I will give in, I think.*

Coach: *Give in to whom?*

Client: *To the part of me that thinks, "I am not worth this."*

Coach: *Let's pause for a moment. Let's really welcome this part. Breathe. And how old does that part of you feel, what age? If you let a number come, what would it be?*

Client: *Twelve.*

Coach: *I'm curious. If we were to introduce this 12-year-old for this moment to your grandfather, what would he say to her?*

Client: (Pauses and then breathes deeply.) *He would say, "It will pass, don't worry. You're more than this."*

Coach: *"It will pass, don't worry. You're more than this." Would this 12-year-old part of you hear him?*

Client: *Yes.*

Coach: *Would she argue with him? Would she try to take trade offs with him?*

Client: *No.*

Coach: *That's good to know. So, I'm really curious right now, because it seems to me, wouldn't it be wonderful if, also, on those walks that you did in the morning that you could facilitate a conversation between that 12-year old part of yourself and your grandfather?*

Client: *Okay.* (Smiles broadly.) *I could. Yes.*

Coach: *And if you could really take this part of yourself with you and your grandfather, how would you remember to do that? What would*

be your way of making sure that for these 3 weeks, I take that walk and they are with me? For example, do you have photographs of your grandfather?

Client: *Yes, I do. I could put his photograph by my bedside so that it is the first thing I see when I wake up.*

Coach: *Great. In order for you to take your walk every morning, about what time would you do it?*

Client: *I would have to get up at seven in the morning.*

Coach: *Let's take a moment and imagine it is 3 weeks from now and you have successfully gone for that walk every morning during that time, taking your grandfather and that 12-year old part of you with you. See what you see, hear what you hear, feel what you feel. How do you feel, now that you've done it 3 weeks?*

Client: (Smiles broadly.) *Great!*

Coach: *Awesome. Looking back now from the future, what has allowed you to be successful?*

Client: *Well, I did it lightly. I didn't think so much. I just got out there and did it, and I enjoyed it.*

Coach: *Enjoyed it, yes. How did you remember to do that as you look back over those 3 weeks, to go lightly, to enjoy?*

Client: *Thinking that I deserve it, thinking positive things. Breathing.*

Coach: *Thinking that you deserve it, and breathing.*

Client: *Thinking of myself, because I forget that.*

Coach: *That's right. Remembering yourself. So, from this place in the future, what would you to say to the you who is getting up each day at 7am?*

Client: *Let's go!*

Coach: *"Let's go!" So, come back here to the present moment right now. Imagine you are waking up at 7am and you see the photograph of your grandfather and then that you in the future, three weeks from now, and she is saying. "Let's go!" What happens?*

Client: (Smiles broadly.) *I feel more inside of myself and solid. I am ready to go.*

Coach: *I see that.*

Client: *Thank you very much. Thank you for helping me so much.*

LET'S GO!

In this demonstration, the coach used a combination of protocols for mental rehearsal, increasing motivation and self-anchoring to support the client to be prepared for and to follow through with a practice developed to bring more balance into her life. We can also see that obstacles can occur at any of the six steps. They don't necessarily wait for step five in order to show up. And they are not all completely taken care of at step five.

In fact, we would go as far as to say that, in some ways, each of the six steps includes all of the six steps. That is, step 1 can end up being a mini version of all six steps; step 2 can end up being a mini version of all six steps; step 3 can be a mini version of all six steps; and so on.

In the next chapter we will be giving an example of putting all six steps together as a single unified process.

Dare to be your own illumination
Trust the energy that courses through you.
Trust, then take surrender even deeper. Be the energy.
Don't push anything away.
Follow each sensation back to its source in vastness and pure presence.
Emerge so new, so fresh, that you don't know who you are.
Welcome in this season of monsoons.
Be the bridge across the flooded river and the surging torrent underneath.
Be unafraid of consummate wonder.
Be the energy, and blaze a trail across the clear night sky like lightning.
Dare to be your own illumination.

~ Dana Faulds

Chapter 9

Putting All Six Steps Together

We are now ready to see how all of the six steps of Generative Coaching fit together in a single process. Typically, one step flows organically into the next step. Of course, every journey is different and the way the steps unfold is unpredictable. That is part of what makes it generative.

In our Generative Coaching training programs, we frequently do a timed demonstration where we will basically take no longer than five minutes for each of the six steps. We consider it a "creative constraint" that creates the possibility of **"disciplined flow."** It also gives the opportunity to show how the 6-steps of Generative Coaching unfold naturally during a session.

The following is a transcript of such a timed demonstration of the six steps that we did together as co-coaches. It provides a good illustration of how the six steps would unfold in an actual coaching session.

Step 1: Open a COACH field

Coach: *We know that there are a multiple ways to create a COACH field. Very often, rather than guide somebody directly to the COACH state, I will start by asking,* **"Have you ever been in a state where you really felt a sense of flow, connection and calm creativity?"**

Client: *Yes. What has just come to my mind is what Stephen calls the three seeds – "stillness," "silence" and "spaciousness." I just imagine dropping each one of these seeds through my whole body and into the ground. Stillness.* (Breathes deeply.) *Silence.* (Breathes deeply.) *And the last one, is spaciousness.* (Breathes deeply.)

Coach: *And as you drop those three seeds, I'm curious what do you notice? What are you aware of that happens inside you?*

Client: *I am connected.* (Places hands over her heart.)

Coach: *And I see you touching your heart area. Is that where you are connected?*

Client: *Yes, and I'm open. I'm present and I'm open.* **(Breathes deeply.)**

Coach: *I see you. Welcome. And on a scale of 0 to 10 right now, where 10 would be "I'm in my best COACH state," and where 0 would be I'm just checked out or CRASHed – where would you say you are?*

Client: *It's seven and a half in the moment.*

Coach: *Seven and a half? That's nice. I am curious what, if anything, might help you just to get a little bit more into your COACH state. What could help you to deepen it a little bit more?*

Client: *I think I need to be a little bit more grounded. Just a little bit more present.* (Breathes deeply.)

Coach: (Breathes deeply.) *I just want to share that with you. It feels good to make what we call a "COACH field." I was joining you in the state created by those seeds, and I was adding having an imaginary kangaroo tail that I could sit, to help me stay grounded and stable.* (Bends knees and breathes deeply.)

Client: (Bends knees and breathes deeply.) *That helps. Now my COACH state is more like eight and a half.*

Step 2: Set Intention/Goal

Coach: *Thank you for bringing those three seeds into the conversation. And we'll be just keeping those seeds on a little shelf here, because we know there will be times during the work that a little CRASH might come up. We now know that we've got these seeds to help us to reconnect with your underlying creative state. What do you think about that?*

Client: (Breathes deeply.) *It sounds good.*

Coach: *Stillness, silence, spacious. So that allows you to begin to sense to the most authentic level in you, if there was one thing that you think it'd be really great to be able to create in your life, what would that be?*

Client: *I really want to bring all the learnings and experiences which have come from my recent studies with Generative Change into my life, and to my work.*

Coach: *That's awesome! I want you to know that when you share from that place, I get this red ball of fire that begins to open in my*

heart. And I'm just curious as to what happens in your body as you begin to speak out with curiosity, compassion, and courage. When you say, "I want to bring those learnings and experiences back into my work and life." Where does that touch you?

Client: *It's touches my heart.* (Places hands over her heart.)

Coach: *That's great! So, welcome. Your creative journey begins from someplace deep in your heart. Welcome. Welcome. And I wonder if you were to make the statement, "I want to bring these learnings and experiences back to my work and home," what would be the somatic model that would lift that out of your belly and your heart and into the world of your work and into your home? What are the words?*

Client: (Breathes deeply and then extends both arms out from her heart as if reaching out to something in front of her.) *Let's do it at last!*

Coach: *Let's do it at last.* (Mirrors her gesture.)

Coach: *And I want to ask you to sense your belly and your heart. We want to make sure that you keep this connection.*

Client: (Extends both arms out from her heart.) *Let's do it at last!*

Coach: *And as you say the words "Let's do it at last!" and make the gesture is there an image that comes to you of what that means to you?*

Client: (Makes the gesture.) *It's some type of spaceship.*

Coach: *So if you were to visualize that spaceship taking off, making the gesture, and saying those words again. What would that be like?*

LET'S DO IT AT LAST!

Client: *Let's do it at last.* (Extends both arms out from her heart.)

Coach: (Mirrors her gesture.) *Let's try that again.*

Client: *Let's do it at last!* (Extends both arms out from her heart.)

Step 3:
Establish a Generative State

Coach: *Step 3 is about the generative state and the basic prototype for generative state is the 3 positive connections – the connection **to your intention**, **to yourself**, and **to your field of resources**. And I'm curious, just right now, as you make that gesture and say those words, on a scale of 0 to 10, how kind of committed and congruent do you feel to that?*

Client: *It is 8. But something is like bumping here.* (Places both hands over her upper chest.)

Coach: *That's part of your team. Welcome. We're glad that you're here. Welcome. And as we make space for whatever is bumping there* (points to her upper chest) *let's remember those seeds of silence, stillness, spaciousness. And let's ground a bit our kangaroo tails.* (Bends knees and breathes deeply.) *Welcome.*

Client: (Bends knees and breathes deeply.) *Welcome. Yes. It is feeling more calm now.*

Coach: *What would you say is the positive intention of this "bumping?"*

Client: *It's just, "You need time for yourself. You need to take care about yourself."*

Coach: *You need time for yourself. To take care about yourself. That is important to remember as you "do it at last." And, in order to bring your learnings and experiences back into your work and home while making sure you have time for yourself, you are going to need some good resources. As you make that gesture of your intention* (extends both arms out from his heart) *and picture that image of the spaceship, if you were to open out to your field of resources, who or what comes to you as being something that will be really significant and important to support you to "do this at last" and remember to take care about yourself?*

Client: (Extends both arms out from her heart.) *That's my ancestors.*

Coach: *Any particular ancestors?*

Client: *Yes, my grandfather and my grandmother.*

Coach: *Your grandfather and your grandmother. How are you aware of their presence as you stand here in this place?*

Client: (Breathes deeply and opens her chest, straightening her shoulders.) *I just feel them to my right and to my left.*

Coach: *How strongly can you feel connected to you grandfather and your grandmother right now on a scale of 0-10?*

Client: *It's nine.*

Coach: *Nine. That's great. And how do you feel that connection to them? Something here?* (Points to her shoulders.)

Client: *Yes. It's like my shoulders started to straighten.* (Breathes deeply.)

Coach: *Welcome.* (Straightens his shoulders and breathes deeply.) *Welcome.*

Step 4: Move Into Action

Coach: *Now, as we begin to move into action and create your storyboard for bringing your learnings and experiences back into your work and home and "doing it at last," while also taking care about yourself, it will be important to have the support of your grandfather and grandmother.*

Client: *Yes, they are here...* (Straightens her shoulders and breathes deeply.)

Coach: *So, what we're going to do is to make a timeline. Which direction is your future?*

Client: *This way.* (Stands on her timeline and faces to her right.)

Coach: *I'm going to ask you to imagine concretely living this path of bringing your learnings and experiences back into your work and home and doing it at last, while also taking care about yourself.* (Extends both arms out from his heart.) *What are the key steps?*

Client: (Extends both arms out from her heart.) *Finding balance.*

Coach: *Finding balance. I am curious, what would that look like in a concrete way? As you have this balance and you're integrating those learnings and experiences, what would a day be like? Concretely, what are you doing? What's happening?*

Client: *Okay. It will be, the first part of the day I really will take care about myself.*

Coach: *How would you do that? What do you do in the first part of the day to take care of you?*

Client: *Go for a walk and do some balancing exercise, like yoga. And spend the morning with the children.*

Coach: *Great. And then?*

Client: *And then in the afternoon start to do client work. There are also some activities related to this online platform I am creating. But it's after noon. Everything after noon.*

Coach: *After noon. That's good to know! That's becoming concrete now. And then what? Do you do client work and Internet platform until midnight?*

Client: *No. Maximum until 8pm.*

Coach: *Maximum until 8pm. And then after 8pm?*

Client: *Spend time with my family.*

Coach: *Spend time with your family. Great. So let's walk through these steps on your timeline very slowly, so that you can get this storyboard in the muscle. In the morning you go for a walk, do some balancing exercise, yoga, spend the morning with the children. Then, after noon, doing client work and activities related to your Internet platform . . .*

Client: (Begins to slowly walk up her timeline, then hesitates.)

Step 5: Transform Obstacles

Coach: *You see right at that point, she hits the obstacle again. So she's going too fast. Her body is giving her feedback that she has not cognitively recognized.*

It seems like you're touching some really core important pieces. You are connecting to that passionate interest to bring your learnings and experiences into your life and work. Only you're discovering that when you do that, it also activates a twin that lives in the basement. So I wonder if we could do just a little process in terms of "I go towards bringing my learnings and experiences back into my work and home" (extends both arms out from his heart) *and then "the other need that I have is . . ." and then just allow whatever other response comes to emerge.*

Client: (Extends both arms out from her heart, pauses and then places both hands over her upper chest.) *Yeah, it's up here.*

Coach: *That's great. That's great! Some other core part says, "I've got to go with you on this journey too."* (Places both hands over his upper chest.) *That's great. You might feel that, even as you bring connection to this part, you really are open to the presence of your grandmother and your grandfather.*

Client: (Straightens her shoulders and breathes deeply.)

Coach: *It is so interesting to learn that as you are enthusiastically bringing your learnings and experiences to the outside world, somebody else who lives deep inside says, "If you're going on that path, I'm coming too." Isn't that great? So let's find what movement, says "Welcome!"*

Client: (Straightens her shoulders and breathes deeply, then places both hands gently over her upper chest.) *Welcome.*

Coach: *If you were to let a number come up for the age of this part of you, what would that be?*

Client: *Seven.*

Coach: *Seven years old. That's awesome. Isn't it great to know that this seven-year old part of you wants to be part of how you bring your learnings and experiences into the world?*

Client: *Yes. I need to remember that she is there.*

Coach: *I'm going to just suggest that you find a 3-part movement. One is that movement of "at last, I am bringing my learnings and experiences into the world."* (Extends both arms out from his heart.) *Then, bringing connection to that almost unbearably vulnerable creative core.* (Places both hands over his upper chest.) *Then asking your body to find a third movement that represents both of them together.*

Client: (Extends both arms out from her heart, then places both hands over her upper chest. Straightens her shoulders and breathes deeply. Repeats the gesture of extending her arms out in front of her and then bringing her hands back over her upper chest until it becomes a rhythmic movement. She then extends her right arm while keeping her left hand on her upper chest. She brings the right hand back to her chest and extends the left arm, moving back and forth between extending one arm while keeping the opposite hand on her chest.)

Coach: (Mirrors her gestures.) *That's right. Awesome!*

Client: (Smiles broadly.) *It seems so easy now. So obvious. So natural.*

Step 6:
Practices for Deepening the Change

Coach: *My feeling is that you have done some really focused, important work. Would you agree?*

Client: *Yes.*

Coach: *So what I get curious about is how you will keep this integration continuing and deepening when you get back home. How many kids do you have?*

Client: *Three.*

Coach: *Three. Wow! I'd need a little time for myself too. So I'm going to ask if you could just take a breath and sense a first practice, a first commitment. You were starting to explore how to bring your learnings and experiences into your professional life and, at the same time, stay nurturing and connected to a deeper, more vulnerable self. If you were to make the statement, "One practice I think would be really helpful might be . . ."* (Extends his right arm while keeping his left hand on his upper chest. Then brings the right hand back to his chest and extends the left arm.) *What comes up as your answer?*

Client: (Extends her right arm while keeping her left hand on her upper chest. She brings the right hand back to her chest and extends the left arm, moving back and forth between extending one arm while keeping the opposite hand on her chest.) *Yoga.*

Coach: *Yoga. That's great. So one thing I really would be inviting you to do after this session is take some time for yourself, write down your thoughts and remember that what came out in terms of one really important way to give you the grounding, the balance and the connection to a deeper sense of yourself as you bring your learnings and experiences into your professional life is yoga. Isn't that great to know?*

Client: *Yes.*

Coach: *And if you tune into that deeper, more vulnerable self,* (places both hands over his upper chest) *what would be the special way to make the commitment, "I'm going to be really good hearted to all four of my children, including that seven-year old inside of me."*

Client: (Places both hands over her upper chest. Breathes deeply and smiles.) *It's taking a walk in the morning. Before doing anything else.*

Coach: *Taking a walk. And we really want to appreciate that in some ways there is a sacred element to this. This place here* (places both hands over his upper chest), *"That's your base."*

Client: (Places both hands over her upper chest. Breathes deeply and smiles.) *Yes. I will take care of her on my morning walk.*

Coach: *I would also encourage one other practice for how you will keep an ongoing connection to your grandfather and your grandmother. What would be your practice to connect to them each day? Yoga is a good way to keep balance, and walking is a good way to take care of your "base." It is also going to be important to keep that connection to those resources that support you. Can you think of a practice that would support that connection?*

Client: *What came to my mind just now is that I can put a picture of them in my room and by my computer. And then, before I go to bed to say, "Thank you for being here with me this day, thank you."*

Coach: *"Thank you.'*

Client: *Yes. I think ending my day with gratitude will be really important.*

Coach: *I agree. Thank you so much.*

Client: *Thank you. Thank you!*

(Applause.)

Reflections on the Demonstration

There are a number of common patterns that showed up in this demonstration. One is that obstacles often begin to emerge at step two. This is a direct expression of what Carl Jung meant by *"enantiodromia."* Not only does everything contain its opposite but everything eventually turns into its opposite. The more I do one thing, the more its opposite is going to come up in an attempt to bring some type of balance. And so, we're always coaching with an ear for both sides. It is also one of the reasons we like to ask for somatic models. They often make it easier to anticipate the type of balancing force that may emerge.

In this case, there was the complement between *"doing for others and bringing something out into the world"* and *"taking care about myself."* The movement that the client made when she was expressing her intention to *"do it at last"* – extending her arms outward from her heart – was a little bit too one-sided. So that means that it is likely going to be followed by its complement: *"I need to take care of me too"* and the gesture of the hands on her upper chest.

The question is, when this happens, are you there to welcome it, or do you say, *"No, we just go forward, forward, forward, forward."* In that case, the part of you that brings you back to your "base" will be a *"negative" symptom"*. That complementing part starts to show up in its CRASH version. If you don't pick those up, they become the deal-breakers.

In the demonstration, the complementing part showed up at the end of step 2 and was welcomed enough that it did not create too much CRASH. The client was able to maintain a strong enough connection to herself and her intention. Of course, it is important to keep in mind that at steps 2 and 3 there is nothing really concrete to respond to yet. That happens at step 4 when we start moving into action. That is the point that *"the rubber hits the road."* It is here that obstacles are likely to begin to become much more activated.

As a generative coach, we assume that the vast majority of people are motivated enough and competent enough to be able to achieve the goals that they are talking about. The client in this demonstration said, *"I want to bring my learnings and experiences back home."* Do you think she's capable of that? Of course she is! So what would stop her is that, as she goes to do it, something on the pathway begins to activate. And it's our relationship and connection to whatever gets activated that makes it either (a) a resource that moves her into a whole next level of her generative being or (b) a problem that takes her down once again. What makes the difference between a really generative coach and other coaches is that you are paying close attention to that.

It is not uncommon for these inner obstacles to have their origin earlier in our personal history. They have formed originally precisely because they were not welcomed and met with a resourceful human presence. This is one of the reasons we will frequently ask about the "age" of the seeming obstacle. We want to humanize it so that the client perceives it as a part of himself or herself rather than as a negative alien presence. As a generative coach, we are not interested in the particular content of what was happening at that age or "why" the pattern has developed. Rather we want to hold that presence in a larger COACH field so that the expression can soften from its current rigid form. Then, by finding its positive intention, we can explore new, more integrated expressions of that part of the client's inner holon.

Of course, this is also where the resources that we gathered at step 3 become essential. They are often what helps to create the bridge between the two seeming polarities and transforms them into generative complementarities.

We do want to point out that there are times when the obstacle creates a significant amount of CRASH before we get to step 5. In those cases, we would just go ahead and use one of our prototypes for transforming obstacles.

And, as usual, we realize that what we did in the session was just opening a possibility. Nothing has changed yet, and nothing will change until you make a commitment to do what you need to do on daily basis to actually make that change happen.

As a coach, it is going to be important to follow up on those practices. *"Are you saying thank you to the grandparents every night? Are you keeping that commitment to go only after noon? Are you taking your morning walk? Are you doing your yoga?"* If not, you need to go back to the storyboard and step 5 to explore more deeply.

So it may seem on the surface, that the session you had should result in some positive change but, when you check after the session, nothing happened or the client didn't follow through. Our basic systemic assumption would be that there is some other presence in the holon that is not being included in the conversation. So it's sabotaging it or taking it down. That means more step 5.

Putting all Six Steps Together

STEP 1: COACH STATE

(WELCOME AND TRANSFORM OBSTACLES WHENEVER THEY APPEAR IN THE PROCESS)

YOU NEED TO TAKE CARE ABOUT YOURSELF!

LET'S DO IT AT LAST!

STEP 2: SET AN INTENTION

STEP 3: ESTABLISH A GENERATIVE STATE

STEP 6:
PRACTICES FOR
DEEPENING THE
CHANGE

STEP 5:
TRANSFORM
OBSTACLES

STEP 4:
MOVE INTO
ACTION

The breezes at dawn has secrets to tell you.
Don't go back to sleep.
You must ask for what you really want.
Don't go back to sleep.
People are going back and forth
across the threshold where the two worlds touch.
The door is round and open.
Don't go back to sleep.

– Rumi

Conclusion

As we pointed out in our introductory chapter, the power of the six-step Generative Coaching model is that it is, on one hand, a very clear step-by-step process. On the other hand, it is not rigid. It allows for both flexibility and the inclusion of many different methods and modalities to satisfy any particular step.

In fact, we are planning future volumes on Generative Coaching in which we will show how to apply different distinctions and other approaches that you can add to enrich each of those steps. One of our motivations for developing the six-step model was that we were trying to figure out a way to put all of our 90 years of combined work into one structure. We have discovered that, within the structure defined by these six steps, we can bring everything we know into a session with a client.

We encourage you to do that too – to engage all your knowledge and talents as you practice these steps. That is how you will become empowered to make the steps your own.

Fundamentally the six steps of Generative Coaching provide a deep and practical way of helping clients to get access to what we are calling the *"quantum field"* of possibilities and expand their potential. The steps are essentially designed to support the conversation between the realm of quantum possibilities and the world of classical reality – between structure and an open field. This is what Rumi refers to as *"the threshold where the two worlds touch."*

The Importance of the Relational Field Between the Coach and Client

Whatever knowledge or tools you are using, however, it is important to remember that it is the quality of the relational field between the coach and client that is, ultimately, the determining factor of whether something really magical is going to happen. The exact same tools will produce a completely different result in different relational fields. We like to point out that if the field holding the interaction is in CRASH, then whatever you think makes no difference, whatever you say makes no difference and whatever you do makes no difference. If the exact same interaction is happening within a COACH field, then whatever you think is magic, whatever say is magic and whatever you do is magic.

Engaging Somatic Intelligence

Another thing we would both continue to reiterate is the importance of involving the body and somatic intelligence in your coaching. Whenever your body is not involved, it is almost impossible to truly be generative. It is necessary to free the body and use the body, because it knows, better than our cognitive minds, how to bring something into this world.

Facilitating the Conversation Between Complementarities

Another one of the main points that we've been emphasizing is that creativity is always a conversation between complementary perspectives and energies. For example, to be effective in the world, we need more than lightness, softness and sweetness. We also need determination and fierceness. If you only have the lightness and sweetness, it is hard to make a commitment that *"this is what I want to do in the world."* This is the Taoist principle of Yin and Yang. When the Yin and the Yang are interconnected, that's where we really make a difference.

However, if one of these soul energies, as it awakens through you, is met with negative human presence, it becomes locked down in a rigid form and appears as an obstacle. For instance, imagine if you grow up being told, *"You must always be good and calm."* How much power do you feel? How much interest? How much self-support do you feel to live your life to the fullest? And then, if you tried to bring some type of determined and fierce balancing energy through you, you were told, *"You can't bring that part of your soul energy into the world."* And you shut it down. Now you live in a one-sided way. And at some point you can't really continue to do that anymore. You realize that it is not enough to *"always be good and calm."* And that is where it is important to understand that your deepest resource is actually the *"evil twin"* that has been locked in the basement for years.

That is why, as generative coach, you are always sensing, *"Where is the energy? What is in that energy field? And what is not in it?"*

Practicing Disciplined Flow

We also want to point out that the six-steps of Generative Coaching, like any methodology that has a generative capacity, is a process of lifelong learning. When we started studying with our mutual mentor Milton Erickson, we were both at the ripe age of 19. It was really clear to both of us that the most important idea in Erickson's legacy – the one that all of his students could agree upon and his great radical contribution – was the notion of *"utilization."* It involved skillfully welcoming every part of a person, and then seeing how to creatively engage with all of these parts so that they could become realized as positive essential contributions for a person's awakening. As the result of that process, some positive pattern would emerge – some new and more effective reorganization of the person's experience.

Over the years, every time that either of us has thought that we finally understood and mastered what Erickson meant by utilization, something would happen that would make us realize that there was much more to it; that utilization was a much deeper and more interesting principle than we had thought. Eventually, we realized that there is no final understanding or mastery of it. You can devote your whole life open-heartedly, deeply, looking to understand the nature of creative utilization, and there is always more to learn.

It has been the same with these 6 steps of Generative Coaching. In the years since we first developed the model, we have continued to learn more and more about: What is COACH state? What is an intention? What is a generative state? What is a good action plan? What does it mean to transform obstacles? What are effective practices that deepen the changes begun in a coaching session? We hope you will approach these steps with that type of creative curiosity as well.

To us, one of the beauties of Generative Change work is that it is a part of a larger lineage that many generations of people have been exploring. And now we are just barely beginning to have an understanding of what it is about; which means that we can get so much more if we just give ourselves to it. Opening to the mystery every day.

Mihály Csíkszentmihályi, also known as *"Dr. Flow,"* maintains that the high performance state of "flow" comes from the balance between discipline and openness. That is the edge that we are always trying to find as coaches. And, from there, to find and work at our client's edge. When you do that, then you find that those are 6 steps are never predictable and boring. There is always another mystery at any step. There is always something more you can keep discovering. Isn't that amazing?

For those of us who will die, wouldn't it be nice to be looking forward to that time, far, far away and many, many years into the future, when you're on that threshold and you could turn to the person next to you and say, *"That was amazing!"* and then drop back into the quantum field. And, if you are like our California ex-governor, your last words might be *"I'll be back."*

We'll be back in our future volumes of *Generative Coaching*.

Afterword

We hope that you have enjoyed this introduction to Generative Coaching. There is much more to learn and explore on this topic, and we are already working on future volumes. If you are interested in more in-depth learning about the principles and applications of Generative Coaching, you may want to consider taking one of our 15-day Generative Coaching Certification courses.

Much of the text in this book, in fact, was taken from transcripts of the first module of Generative Coaching Certification programs done in London, St. Petersburg and Cologne. Certification in Generative Coaching qualifies you for professional membership in the **International Association for Generative Change** (IAGC) as a *"Practitioner of Generative Change in Generative Coaching."*

The International Association for Generative Change

We established the International Association for Generative Change in 2013 as a means to build a global community of people who were passionate about exploring, practicing and developing applications of Generative Change. IAGC is an international association that supports Generative Change practitioners, training organizations and certification programs throughout the world; providing international standards, a code of ethics and a platform for exchange. The vision at the foundation of IAGC is a world where people around the planet are empowered and awakened to creatively meet the challenges of our time by living the principles of Generative Change.

The IAGC offers professional membership, associate membership and other resources that promote Generative Change in personal, professional and organizational contexts. The IAGC website serves as a virtual hub which brings together people from all over the world to meet, exchange, collaborate and develop new applications of Generative Change work. IAGC also sponsors a yearly international conference which includes master classes, mastermind groups, generative conversations and networking opportunities focused on topics relating to the application of generative change in different areas.

A key goal of the IAGC is to bring principles of Generative Change to multiple professions. As we pointed out in Chapter 2, there are three main areas of application of generative change work: (1) Generative Coaching, (2) Generative Trance and (3) Generative Change in Business. IAGC was established in order to support its members to bring new models

and methods to diverse communities and professions. Its ultimate purpose is to help create a world where coaches, psychotherapists, leaders, teachers, trainers and entrepreneurs facilitate principles and processes of generative change in many contexts: individual change, cultural and cross-cultural change, and systemic change in companies and communities.

To learn more about Generative Coaching Certification programs, the International Association for Generative Change and professional or associate membership go to: http://www.generative-change.com

As we have previously mentioned, we both also have our separate, yet related, areas of work and development. Steve has been developing a body of work called "Creative Mind." Robert has a number of projects that apply Neuro-Linguistic Programming and Success Factor Modeling.

For more information about Steve's individual activities, go to:

http://www.stephengilligan.com

http://gilligan-creative.com/

For more information about Robert's individual activities, go to:

http://www.robertdilts.com

http://www.diltsstrategygroup.com

Bibliography

Books

* Bateson, G. (1972), **Steps to an Ecology of Mind**, New York: Ballantine Books.

* Bandler, R. and Grinder, J. (1975), **The Structure of Magic, Volume I**, Palo Alto, Science and Behavior Books.

* Bandler, R. and Grinder, J. (1976), **Patterns of the Hypnotic Techniques of Milton H. Erickson, M.D., Volume** I, Capitola, Meta Publications.

* Csíkszentmihályi, M. (1991), **Flow: The psychology of optimal experience,** New York: Harper Perennial.

* Csíkszentmihályi, M. (1996), **Creativity: Flow and the Psychology of Discovery and Invention**. New York: Harper Perennial.

* Dilts, R. (2003), **From Coach to Awakener**, Santa Cruz: Dilts Strategy Group.

* Dilts, R. (2015-2017), **Success Factor Modeling, Volumes I-III**, Santa Cruz: Dilts Strategy Group.

* Dilts, R., Delozier, J. & Bacon Dilts, D. (2010), **NLP II: The Next Generation**, Santa Cruz: Dilts Strategy Group.

* Dilts, R. & McDonald, R. (1997), **Tools of the Spirit,** Santa Cruz: Dilts Strategy Group.

* Dilts, R. (1990), **Changing Belief Systems With NLP,** Santa Cruz: Dilts Strategy Group.

* Dilts, R. & DeLozier, J. (2000), **Encyclopedia of Systemic Neuro-Linguistic Programming and NLP New Coding**, Santa Cruz: NLP University Press.

* Erickson, M. H. (1980), **The Collected Papers of Milton H. Erickson**; New York: Irvington Publishers Inc.

* Gendlen, E. (1978), **Focusing,** New York: Bantam.

* Gilligan, S. (2012). **Generative Trance: The experience of creative flow**, Carmathen, Wales: Crown House Books.

* Gilligan, S. (1997). **The courage to love: Principles and Practices of Self Relations Psychotherapy,** New York: Norton Professional Books.

* Gilligan, S. (1987). **Therapeutic Trances: The cooperation principle in Ericksonian hypnotherapy**. New York: Brunner/Mazel.

* Gilligan, S., & Dilts, R. (2009), **The Hero's Journey: A Voyage of Self-Discovery**, Carmathen, Wales: Crown House Books.

* Goswami, A. (1993). **The Self-Aware Universe: How Consciousness Creates the World**, New York: Tarcher/Putnam.

* Haley, J. (1973), **Uncommon Therapy: The Psychiatric Techniques of Milton H. Erickson, M.D.**, New York: W. W. Norton & Co.

* Jung, C., G., (1961), **Collected Works of C. G. Jung**, Princeton, Princeton University Press.

* Koestler, A. (1964), **The Act of Creation: A study of the conscious and unconscious in science and art**, New York: Macmillan

* Levine, P. (2010). **In an unspoken voice: How the body releases trauma and restores goodness,** Berkeley, CA: North Atlantic Books.

* McGilchrist, I. (2009). **The Master and His Emissary. The Divided Brain and the Making of the Western World,** New Haven: Yale University Press.

* Moss, R. (2007), **The Mandala of Being: Discovering the Power of Awareness**, Novato: New World Library.

* Osbon, D. (1991), **Reflections on the Art of Living; A Joseph Campbell Companion.** New York: HarperCollins.

* Sapolsky, R. (1988), **Why Zebras Don't Get Ulcers: An Updated Guide To Stress, Stress Related Diseases, and Coping**, New York: W. H. Freeman.

* Ware, B. (2011), **The Top Five Regrets of the Dying: A Life Transformed by the Dearly Departing**, Bloomington, Balboa Press.

* Wilber, K. (2001), **A Brief History of Everything**, Boston: Shambhala.

* Wilhelm, H., Jung, C, (1967), translated by Baynes, C., **I Ching, the Book of Changes**, Princeton, Princeton University Press.

About the Authors

Robert Dilts

Stephen Gilligan

Antonio Meza:
Illustrator

Robert Dilts   Stephen Gilligan

Robert B. Dilts

Robert Dilts has been a developer, author, trainer and consultant in the field of Neuro-Linguistic Programming (NLP) – a model of human behavior, learning and communication – since its creation in 1975 by John Grinder and Richard Bandler. Robert is also co-developer (with his brother John Dilts) of Success Factor Modeling and (with Stephen Gilligan) of the process of Generative Change. A long time student and colleague of both Grinder and Bandler, Mr. Dilts also studied personally with Milton H. Erickson, M.D. and Gregory Bateson.

In addition to spearheading the applications of NLP to education, creativity, health, and leadership, his personal contributions to the field of NLP include much of the seminal work on the NLP techniques of Strategies and Belief Systems, and the development of what has become known as Systemic NLP. An author more than 25 books, some of his techniques and models include: Reimprinting, the Disney Imagineering Strategy, Integration of Conflicting Beliefs, Sleight of Mouth Patterns, The Spelling Strategy, The Allergy Technique, Neuro-Logical Levels, The Belief Change Cycle, The SFM Circle of Success and the Six Steps of Generative Coaching (with Stephen Gilligan).

A co-founder of Dilts Strategy Group, Robert is also co-founder of NLP University International, the Institute for Advanced Studies of Health (IASH) and the International Association for Generative Change (IAGC). Robert has a degree in Behavioral Technology from the University of California at Santa Cruz.

Robert Dilts   Stephen Gilligan

Stephen Gilligan, PhD

A seminal American psychologist specializing in creative change.

For over 40 years Dr. Gilligan has been writing, practicing therapy, coaching, and teaching all over the world. Considered one of the great hypnotherapists, his work has expanded far beyond the Ericksonian approach...

Stephen was one of the original NLP students at UC Santa Cruz; Milton Erickson and Gregory Bateson were his mentors. After receiving his psychology doctorate from Stanford University, he became one of the premier teachers and practitioners of Ericksonian hypnotherapy. This work unfolded into his original approaches of Self-Relations and Generative Self, and then further (in collaboration with Robert Dilts) into Generative Coaching. These different traditions have all been updated and integrated into the present Generative Change Work, which includes the applications of Generative Coaching, Generative Psychotherapy, Generative Trance, Hero's Journey, and Systemic Change work.

Stephen has taught in many cultures and countries over the past 30 years, and has published extensively. His books include *The Hero's Journey: A Voyage of Self Discovery* (co-authored with Robert Dilts), the classic *Therapeutic Trances*, *The Courage to Love*, *The Legacy of Erickson*, *Walking in Two Worlds* (with D. Simon), and *Generative Trance: The Experience of Creative Flow*. His forthcoming books are the *Generative Coaching* series (co-authored with Robert Dilts).

Antonio Meza is an architect of vision, supporting entrepreneurs and leaders around the world to communicate complex ideas in a simple and fun way through illustrations, cartoons, or through structuring presentations, books, or websites.

A native of Pachuca, Mexico, Antonio is a Master Practitioner and a Trainer of Neuro-Linguistic Programming (NLP). He has a degree in Communication Sciences from Fundación Universidad de las Américas Puebla, a Masters degree in Film Studies from Université de Paris 3 –Sorbonne Nouvelle, a diploma in Cinema Scriptwriting from the General Society of Writers in Mexico (SOGEM), and a diploma in Documentary Films from France's École Nationale des Métiers de l'Image et du Son (La Fémis). He is also certified in the three levels of the SFM system.

He worked in Mexico as a freelance filmmaker and participated in animated cartoons startups before moving to France where he works as a consultant, coach, and trainer, specializing in storytelling, creative thinking and collective intelligence.

Antonio is also an experienced public speaker member of Toastmasters International. In 2015 he was awarded best speaker at the International Speech Contest of District 59, covering South-West Europe, and reached the semifinals at international level.

He has illustrated 15 books including the 3 volumes of the *Success Factor Modeling* series with Robert Dilts, and now the *Generative Coaching* series with Robert Dilts and Stephen Gilligan.

He also uses his skills as a cartoonist and trainer to collaborate in seminars, conferences and brainstorming sessions as a graphic facilitator, and to produce animated videos to explain complex information in a clear and fun way.

Antonio lives in Paris with his wife Susanne, his daughter Luz Carmen and his cats *Ronja* and *Atreju*.

For more visit:

www.antoons.net

www.linkedin.com/in/antoniomeza/

Contact Antonio: hola@antoons.net

Generative Coaching

Lightning Source UK Ltd.
Milton Keynes UK
UKHW020715270421
382702UK00004B/20

9 780578 896960